PLAY DIRECTION

for the

HIGH SCHOOL THEATRE

Other Books by John Wray Young

The Community Theatre and How It Works

How to Produce the Play

Audition Scenes for Students—Volume One

Directing The Play

Community Theatre—A Manual for Success

Audition Scenes for Students—Volume Two

John Wray Young

PLAY DIRECTION

for the

HIGH SCHOOL THEATRE

KENNIKAT PRESS • *1973*
Port Washington, N. Y. • London

Library of Congress Catalog Card No: 73-78885

ISBN: 0–8046–9040–5

Manufactured in the United States of America

Published by
Kennikat Press, Inc.
Port Washington, N.Y. / London

For John Wray Latell

Born the year before this book —
He is our second grandson.

CONTENTS

PROLOGUE

I do not know of a living author of books on theatre who has been as fortunate as I in receiving continuing enthusiasm and appreciation for his six volumes. I have deeply appreciated this and yet feel that this seventh book is the most needed.

For a dozen years the Youngs have felt attention needed to be paid once again to the ancient and immutable law of cause and effect, particularly in relation to young people and the American theatre. Partially the neglect of this law may be attributed to the popularity of the first word, with a capital C of course, and pluralized. As any proper watcher of television can tell you, if a prominent film or tape actor doesn't have a personal Cause, his or her agent will create one to suit.

Many Causes are fine, and some even have money left over for the purpose after administrative costs have been paid. Yet not much is said about the Effect of the Cause upon the adherent. In too many cases this force turns back on the doer; if the Cause involves negation, hate, downgrading, the ultimate result may yield more change in the followers than in the target. The act, to use the noun rather than the verb transitive, tends to determine what we are. Playwrights know this, that the acts of a life mold the character. Actors are aware, at times subconsciously, that the portrait they create on the face with makeup is the picture of a life.

It is regrettable that so many years need pass before a person realizes that what he is results from his actions, far more than from the actions done to him. Effect so often turns back upon he who acts. If we injure someone purposely in anger, the victim hopefully may heal, but the aggressor is bound to suffer some permanent disfigurement. The great danger is that violence, either mental or physical, is infectious and tends to continue with increasing damage to the individual.

I trust you agree that seldom, in our brief two centuries of nationhood, have we had decades where our young people as desperately needed lines of action which are positive, optimistic, creative. As the second, and major, reason for this book, never has the living theatre in the United States so urgently needed assurance that definite and logical steps are being taken to make its tomorrow better.

You see, the theatre also is the victim of our inverse formula of cause and effect. In recent years it so often has been sacrificed on the popular Altar of Causes. We have seen play after play, chiefly produced on Manhattan Island, devoted to protest, pornography, nudity, politics; written not with those forces as a starting point for a true aesthetic experience, but rather as vehicles designed to carry only the Cause itself. Historically the play form always has refused to play the harlot; it would not be prostituted by the wrong raison d'etre. Few periods in twenty–five centuries have witnessed such debauchery as we have known. We may take some small comfort in looking at our bookshelves and noting that the only manuscripts in these categories which survive in playable form are those written with adherence to theatre's dominant purpose, to give civilized man an aesthetic experience which might add to his stature. If there is no enduring benefit from the communion of emotional experience—the only reason theatre has lived so long—we'd best ring down our curtains and leave the whole business of entertaining America to the cultural giants of film and tape and stock–car races and roller derbies and . . .

But we don't want to do that and perhaps we won't if we can get certain positive forces moving more intelligently. One of the most important of these is the high school theatre. It is not easy to convince a teenager that life can be a long and joyful experience *if* one holds to proper values. Our colleagues of television say it succinctly with a one–minute Public Service spot.

The man is sitting in his comfortable room, listening to music, reading a book. As the voice-over speaks, the objects named disappear. "If you take away Man's books, his paintings, his music, his art and his Theatre, he finds himself again up a tree." And sure enough the figure, now looking quite apelike, is sitting in a tree; ten million years of progress are gone.

A few chapters of this book have appeared in *Dramatics Magazine* and their reception in three thousand high schools has made me eager to have the entire work reach the nearly thirty thousand schools which each year do plays in the fifty states.

Happily, our inverse formula of cause and effect works equally well on the other side of the street. Those who make theatre properly, with dedication and well directed talent, always receive more from the experience than they give. The way to this happy confluence of values will be found in the pages ahead.

But as you travel the exciting road through play selection, casting, rehearsal, and the intricate techniques of directing, keep in mind that properly produced theatre needs must travel a two–lane highway. A play may be directed splendidly but there is not likely to be success unless the technical side of the production is executed on *its* timetable.

The third of our books, *How to Produce the Play,** was written to provide a comprehensive guide to the technical side of theatre. It is perhaps the most complete writing on modern and economical stagecraft as opposed to the archaic "permanent scenery" methods still taught in too many colleges and universities. It treats of all stagecraft elements from backstage organiza-

---

* Young, Margaret Mary and John Wray Young. *How to Produce the Play.* Dramatic Publishing Co. 1970.

tion through design, building, properties, sound effects, costumes, makeup and lighting. It is an ideal companion to the new book you now hold in your hands. Reference is made to it again in Chapter Six.

I wish you increasing good fortune with each play you do for they have great importance. You may have heard me say before and you will hear me say again—I believe that much of the hope for America's Theatre of Tomorrow lies in the quality of high school drama.

PLAY DIRECTION
for the
HIGH SCHOOL THEATRE

chapter one

A POVERTY PROGRAM
FOR HIGH SCHOOL THEATRE

High school theatre is the poverty area among American artistic endeavors. Ill–housed, ill–fed and desperately lacking
properly trained leadership, this enterprise touches the lives of
millions of teen–aged pupils but often either leaves no lasting
impression or results in an experience–impact of the wrong kind.

Play production in the secondary schools rarely enjoys one–
tenth the interest or support given vociferously to the athletic
program—and in rare (but fortunate) schools may enjoy one–
fifth of the success and security enjoyed by music. All this, mind
you, a half–century after play–production gained in many places
the minimum and meager academic rating of an activity.

The stark truth is that today a majority of high school productions are one–time stunts, lacking connection with a sustain-
ed program and bearing no resemblance to an enriching learning
experience.

Considering the prestigious problems which face the new generation—and, don't forget, they also face the old—as the twentieth century flees headlong toward the twenty–first, does it really matter what is the end result of all the time, the talent and the energy consumed in the production of thirty or forty–thousand plays each year in our high schools? With all the causes and difficulties which confuse the world around us, should we not rejoice that here is an enterprise for the young in which there is fun in the doing, and which offers such a splendid final reward as a picture in the yearbook. Who wants to look for significance in what many principals and schools boards consider patently to be an extracurricular frill? In the area of teen–age living shall we not be content with the things that really matter, such as having a championship football team or seeing that the marching band does get those ten–thousand dollar uniforms? At a time when the adult American theatre largely has fumbled its way to the verge of that last step over the brink of despair, who has the right to trouble our children's long–haired heads with the disturbing thought that presenting a play could have a profound effect on the future lives of all those involved as practictioners or spectators? Who would have the audacity to suggest that a properly conceived and splendidly executed national program of high school play production could help shape the form and meaning of tomorrow's American theatre?

"What a drag! Last year we had fun doing *My Fair Lady;* next year we'll have even more fun doing *It's a Bird, It's a Plane, It's Superman.* Who wants meaning? Who wants purpose? Strum the guitars and squeal." Is that the murky sense of many voices?

Well, I think some seek meaning and many want purpose. A good share of those enlightened may be reading these pages, for I have been speaking of the majority, that placid plurality found in various endeavors who are content with the easy and the obvious. Because so many, of all ages, are eager to wrap themselves ever more snugly in the comfortable, but sterile, cocoons of uninvolvement and non–assumption of responsibility, a new and heavy duty presents itself to the minority: the quality of tomorrow's citizen partially may depend on them.

Shall we consider some of my indictments? I have said that

the high school theatre is "ill–housed." I hardly can wait to hear from all those school boards and the affluent architects who have created their every wish. "Why, we built four high schools in the last two years and every one of those auditoriums (no classic Latin plural here!) has three thousand of the best seats money can buy; and one of them has a stage big enough to play basketball on." And a boast from a Western state, "Our new high school auditorium is a real money–saver—it serves also as a gymnasium!"

In Wisconsin and Indiana I heard, "We spared no expense. I tell you that new school auditorium has the best footlights and borderlights the salesman had in his catalogue." How many authoritative architectural voices have said, "The principle function of the auditorium in the new school is for assembly programs. Further, we think it well suited to band concerts; the two thousand, seven hundred seats are excellently arranged for viewing purposes."

To this and much more such witness, I can agree—in sorrow. Every word is painfully true. The building of high schools accelerates across the fifty states and in many cases they are efficient structures, occasionally even attractive, wherein classes may be taught, meals prepared and served, bands rehearsed, sports practiced and other functions performed, some of them educational.

But where is any consideration of the needs of living theatre? We do not expect building committees to know greatly of acoustics—it is still largely a dusky realm of chance—but surely most architectural firms designing auditoria have stumbled across the fact that communication by the voice of the living actor deteriorates rapidly at a point projected forty feet from the curtain line into the audience.

A scattering of interviews with experienced professional actors who have, on tour, been forced to perform in a typical high school cavern will reveal their experiences were shattering and traumatic. And don't bother me with any words about amplification. The moment you insert microphones between the actors in a play and those innocent citizens who have paid money for seats a hundred feet from the stage, you have a bastard condition which is neither theatre, motion picture, nor even big-screen television.

But if we're stuck with the caverns, what do we do? If you are doomed to the assembly hall, get out the tapeline and use only seats lying in the area between the curtain line and the forty–foot limit of true audibility. "But we'd have to give the play several nights to get the people in!" That would be excellent —a definite step toward real theatre training for your youthful players.

Once you bring your audience down from those soaring balconies and push them to the front of the lower floor, exciting things begin to happen. They may even be freed from the anti-aesthetic experience of staring down this great diminishing wind tunnel, which is the over–all form of so many old and new auditoria, and may find themselves looking at a close–up of actors acting. They can be seen and they can be heard, two basic requirements for the existence of living theatre. With the play as the dominant visual stimulus, your good ticket–buyers may even forget those awful gargoyles and trappings which decorate so many auditorium walls and which competed successfully for their attention when they were seated further back in the expanding reaches of the wind tunnel.

We know, of course, that all this is prologue, for the working area is where the play is created. It is nearly always worse than the auditorium. I know, I know, the principal says you cannot put stage–screws or nails into that shining floor. I have inspected scores of high school stages, and I firmly believe that any architect who specifies a hardwood stage floor either knows nothing of play production or doesn't like what he knows. We see that the proscenium arch is sixty, fifty or if we're lucky, forty feet wide. That the average Broadway house is thirty–four feet apparently never interests the designer of a high school stage.

In the corner, usually opposite the curtain control, is the switchboard which turns the border lights and footlights on and off in all their splendor of red, white and blue. The businessmen who serve on school boards would not dream of buying a machine for their office or factory without consulting the best specialist they could find, but they will approve the purchase of the most expensive machine for the new high school stage, the lighting equipment, with no more research than the word of a traveling salesman from a jobber down the road. The leading lighting equipment companies are eager to bring the truth and to sell fine products, but how many building committees ever bother to ask?

These impossible and perverse conditions found in nearly all high school situations may be among the reasons, perhaps subconscious, why so many high school directors have compromised by presenting pallid replicas of the half–million dollar Broadway musicals. At least they use a lot of bodies which fill the enormous stages. The youngsters don't sing very well, but they are loud, and the high school orchestra or band is also loud. The total effect is at least audible and visible pretty far back in the two thousand, seven hundred seats. But the end result has little to do with our special concern, the creation of living theatre plays in the secondary schools.

In my interviews with high school teachers I was distressed to find that many thought that "ill housing" was the great difficulty, for this problem can be solved, and rather quickly. A simple expedient is to find a large room where productions can be done arena style—and at once the gain in communication, emotional involvement, repeated performances is apparent. Again, a room and a platform can become an exciting experience in thrust staging. Bad as it seems, housing is almost the least of our difficulties.

Shall we consider two really formidable matters, the first justifying my phrase, "ill–fed"? Into the meandering stream of high school drama there has never poured a sufficient number of properly trained directors; a most generous estimate in some years would demand the use of trickle. In convention speeches I have heard some of my colleagues use, as if it were an old joke, the story of the principal who said, "Last year I had the chemistry teacher do the senior play, so this year I'll assign it to the math teacher."

Regrettably it is an old story, but it continues in hundreds of cities and towns today—which makes it very unfunny. This whimsical approach indicates an administrative viewpoint that

the intricate and difficult process of sound play production involves no more technique than monitoring a study hall. It is not
really the principal's fault. He is unknowing because the people
who should have informed him have failed in their jobs. These
are the thousands who earn their living in the university and college educational theatre. In 1936 play production had edged its
way sufficiently into higher education to justify the formation of
the American Educational Theatre Association. Its first duty was
obviously to itself; to justify its presence in the curriculum and to
provide housing and staff for its own needs. In feathering its own
nest, the college theatre succeeded beautifully and today is the
best housed, the most prolifically staffed and the most completely subsidized theatre activity in the United States.

Its second obligation, once ensconced in splendor, was to
properly train people for the needs of all phases of the American
theatre. Here largely it has failed. Many of the professors, having moved comfortably from student to teacher in the unreal
world of academic theatre, continue to think that they should
try to train actors for the commercial theatre. This is a product
so greatly in supply in both New York and Hollywood that
Ralph Bellamy said when he was President of Actors Equity,
"The 1,200 new cards issued this year means simply 1,200 more
broken hearts."

The two areas of dramatic production which have begged for
proper leadership through the years, the high schools and the
community theatres, have never made their point with the professors for a simple late–twentieth century reason. As we all
know, the population explosion in our land has been exceeded
by the acceleration of the college population. Eagerly seizing
the benefits of this accretion, though I've always suspected that
mere bigness in universities was an impugned blessing, the
drama departments have been able to absorb the best of their
product into their own personnel. This in–breeding has resulted
in many institutions in viewpoints so parochial that words like
"high school theatre" and "community theatre directors" make
no contact. After the stare, the conversation fondly turns to
such warmer topics as foundation grants and salary raises.

For the occasional talented drama graduate who happens to

take a high school position, usually through exigency, the kindly chairman of the department has consolation, "Keep your chin up—we'll get you a college job in a year or two."

Verily the high school theatre is most ill fed by the source which should have long provided it with talented and inspired leadership.

The felony is compounded by the attitude and lack of theatre knowledge of the high school principals and education boards. Faced with the monumental problem of building enough classrooms and hiring sufficient staff for the important subjects, they hardly can be blamed for failing to develop a fringe area which so few teachers want to exploit. They can see no economic sense in theatre education for they know that commercial production continues to diminish. The money to be made by a high school play is insignificant, save when it can be seized for the benefit of another activity. In an age basically pragmatic, to devote space and money to an experience which may only result in making the teen–ager a more civilized adult brings no enthusiastic vote from the computers. We are moving expensively, and placidly, down the highway at the end of which we may be the most schooled and least educated nation in history.

School boards are, after all, successful politically; they did get elected, and they know that the average voter will back the athletic program, particularly if the football team is a consistent winner, and will even favor money for music so long as the marching band becomes more antic and gaudier with the passing years. Even a choral group which can entertain the civic clubs makes sense.

To most of these solid citizens in command, theatre has no meaning beyond the badly done senior play they were in or saw. As adults they may have had some contact with a poor, fair or good community playhouse but it seems to have little relationship with what goes on occasionally on that distant stage in the high school auditorium. Become excited about providing suitable housing, staff and money for high school theatre? Not today, thank you!

In this secondary school climate where produced theatre may, at best, find the high privilege of toleration, is it possible that our case does have merit? Many of us are dedicated to its potential and it is well for us to look again for affirmation in unexpected places. Of late our physiologists and sociologists have been saying more and more about the essential value of early learning. Our government is backing these manifestoes with millions for such projects as the Head Start Program. We are being given to understand that first learnings and impressions are the factors which largely determine the ultimate human being.

Parallel with this concern for the shaping of the young is a new factor in the American life pattern. Having more lives, and increasing the length of them, while at the same time new machines do more and more of our work, the nation begins to face up to the challenging fact that our people may soon have more leisure than work years in their expectancy. We are nearing the point where a man's talents and hobbies will dominate his ultimate quality, rather than his skills in craft or profession. I've been saying for some years that I want tomorrow's citizen to find more in this gift of time than bowling, bridge, golf, or even watching three–dimensional television.

It is not easy to see over the curve of time's horizon, but if we can visualize life in America when the market place must be shared for perhaps a twenty–hour work week and a twenty–five–year work life, where the candy of waste–time sports and games becomes oversweet and finally nauseating, then we realize that any move toward creating truly beneficial values in leisure activity is worth the time and the struggle.

The glory that was Greece left us more than some great plays, imposing statuary and noble ruins; it showed that the Arts, as a popular and vital civic force, could add a precious fourth dimension to man's civilization and could raise the quality of his city far beyond its function as a place to eat, sleep and work.

Even in the Athens of twenty–four centuries ago not all citizens could participate successfully in the Arts, since talent is a prerequisite for the true artist, but the Greek theatre did come close to involving all the citizens either as participants or spectators. Perhaps it is the broad invitation of the playhouse which leads some to call it "man's most human art."

The original Olympics were, I'm certain, most exciting and

stirred the populace, but I hazard a guess that the mighty words of the Greek playwrights, entertaining and moving the thousands on the hillsides, did more to improve the quality of the citizenry of Athens.

So now we possess our great machine of education for all and find it geared most generally to the practical matters of science and business. I read and hear, over and over again, the rather frightening words, "The reason you want to go to college is so you can make more money." But the finest experts insist that the Leisure Age lies just a bit beyond our trips to the moon; so the work of preparation should have started yesterday, and high school theatre should be an integral part of that preparation.

Touching, that man so often approaches formidable tasks with the stars in disarray. We want to broaden the scope and improve the quality of living theatre in secondary education when most current aesthetic factors seem diametrically opposed. The dress, the mores and the avocational interests of our teen–agers seem more hopeless to the oldsters than they did to Horace when he contemplated the youth of his day. Yet the young have always had to suffer the agonies of growing up, and they have always done it in wonderful and provoking ways.

We cannot entirely discount their disapproval of the world we seem to have built and invented for them. After all they didn't start the wars or create the bombs—but under their gestures of protest is, many believe, a real hunger for a better, safer and happier milieu. Public taste in avocations is not a matter for great pride in the first of the 1970's. We have been very busy leveling people and principles, and the leveling process, in history both ancient and contemporary, seems to lead downward, not up. Can anyone prove that the quality of television, motion pictures, theatre and literature is better, or better for our citizens, than it was a decade ago? If public taste is the cumulative result of experience and example, then the increasing amount of inadequate, inartistic and often trashy stimuli quite logically continues to depress it.

The current entertainment vogue of S.S.V.—Shock, Sex and Violence—cannot be easily stemmed; but certainly the educational system should be in the forefront of the struggle. A better high school theatre may seem a fragile weapon in the fight to return man to a desire for the Good, the True and the Beautiful, but it can, with other factors, begin to slow the trend and, hopefully, one day reverse it.

It is too pretentious a dream to hope that play production ever can reach the magnitude and influence of the high school athletic program—and yet, in time, if proper techniques and sufficient manpower are used, it conceivably might attain the strength and impact of music. An obvious handicap is our lateness; we are four or five decades behind the coaches and the music people. Who among you is so old that in your youth these dicta were not heard: "The young need physical fitness" and "Every child a music pupil." They are woven into the fabric of America as indelibly as Motherhood and Apple Pie.

We have no real quarrel with the virtues of the precepts. Would that our teen–agers today did spend more time in the playing fields and less in their automobiles. And the principle of universal music lessons is aesthetically good, save that not all children possess a talent in music, as so many cringing neighbors can attest. Years ago I pleaded for a speed–up in developing effective talent measurements for children in writing, sculpture, poetry, painting, design, acting and dance. What might our achievements be in these fields today had the children with those potential talents been pointed to the proper training programs in grade school years rather than continuing with the herd, pounding keyboards and scraping violins? One day these tests will come, and the resulting artists, beginning the long, hard development in early childhood, may enrich our nation even more than those today who move shining into their careers, approved by measurement tests which declare them qualified to operate computers.

Until that literate day of sound Measurement of Art Talent for the child, what immediate blows can we strike for high school theatre? Certainly a priority is the education of the educators. Involve the principal and the school board in your work, impress them with fine productions. With skill you can show that theatre training improves self–confidence, communication, imagination, self–reliance, speech, posture and other benefits essential to the truly developed adult.

Enlightening the college drama and speech departments as to their duty to high school drama and community theatre is equally difficult, and just as vital. It may be that as younger men move up to the chairmanships, some will not be content with the smug path of teaching college teachers to teach college teachers to teach college teachers.

High school theatre's potential for shaping tomorrow's citizen for the new Age of Leisure is tremendous. In time it could reach a majority of teen–agers and instill a lasting appetite for the experience of theatre. This, I hold, could enrich the United States of the twenty–first century.

A substantial part of a citizenry working in and enjoying the Arts not only improves the environment for all, but also makes of themselves more completely civilized beings.

We revere the glory that was Greece. It could happen again. High school theatre could help bring it about. A long and difficult task? Certainly. But a challenge that deserves the best of you and you and you.

chapter two

HOW DIRECTING BEGINS

When the moment arrives that the wish, suggestion or directive is finalized and you realize you are committed to produce a play, you quite understandably may look helplessly about and say, "But I've never directed!"

Go ahead and say it several times if it seems to help, but don't feel any sense of loneliness in your situation. I cannot dredge up a statistic to comfort you but would guess, with the present high school pattern and the volunteer–director system which predominates in community theatre, that possibly a majority of the productions in those two classifications are directed by "first–timers." The estimate may be overly generous, yet if but a third, or even a fourth, of these countless thousands of productions are so administered, it remains a matter of great concern for the present—and the future—of the American theatre to see if we cannot point the way to better direction.

Perhaps the magnitude of the company you keep gives solace, and you're ready for some self-examination, a logical self–scrutiny which may reveal both qualities which will help you learn directing and some characteristics which may hinder.

Finding the positive factors and talents, you can plan their development and guide their progress. Discovering the negative elements is almost equally important because, once unearthed they may be controlled and some of the disasters which befall directors may be avoided.

I'm sure you thought my first question would be, "How much living theatre have you seen?" and you didn't particularly want to answer, "Not very much." Or you may have felt the logical initial inquiry should have been, "How much acting have you done?" and you were all ready with the quick—and brief—reply, "One play in high school and two in college."

These two questions are rather far down my list, for directing is much more than telling a player how to make a gesture. Remember that in the "bad old days" the only procedure remotely connected with modern direction was for generations of actors to pass on to each other "traditional business;" "Macbeth always uses this gesture on that line because Macready did it first that way."

Suppose we start with this: "What do you like in Art?" Yes, Art in general, and then we can move on to specifics. You are a teacher and that means you've gone to school for sixteen or more years. That long journey of cultural adventure exposed you to much of the best in literature, music, painting and perhaps some theatre. In retrospect I'm sure you feel that your tastes changed; what was very exciting in your high school years may have paled in contrast to more significant discoveries your aesthetic senses made in college. If it has been some time since college, you may look backward and think, "My taste in music was so different when I was an undergraduate." Perhaps you can substitute in the same statement the other words: painting, literature, theatre. The word which interests me, however, is "different." I don't think you had a different taste in any of the arts; rather your taste was at a different stage of development.

This is a vital point in the maintenance of civilization: that there be a measurable distance between the aesthetic judgments and values of the adolescent and of the adult. Of course each generation is positive that never before have the young people liked such horrible music, done such ridiculous dances or wanted to read such trashy stories. We can be even more positive that this is a continuing problem of mankind; as you know the Greeks worried a lot about it and wrote down some of their worries.

The real concern of each generation should be with the adults whose tastes remain in adolescence; we find examples in those of mature years whose sole reading is comic books. In some cases this aesthetic immaturity may result from physical incapacity, but many times I fear it happens because in the school years there was no effective series of stimuli to open the doors and reveal the vistas of the arts. Good teaching implies more than inducing youngsters to remember the answers long enough to write them on examination papers.

Thus the teacher dealing in the arts in a secondary school situation must walk an extremely narrow tightrope. At precisely the time when we must let youth be young and enjoy without guilt the current fads in music, dancing and literature, we have to stimulate so skillfully, and guide so subtly, that the first tastes of the more adult pleasures in the arts will impart a lasting appetite which will grow and broaden with maturity.

This brings us right back to you and the difference you feel in your tastes as you compare youth and adulthood. Taking inventory, you may find you like both the traditional and the modern in painting, except "I don't find meaning in much of the avant–garde work." Don't let that make you feel narrow, for a good bit of the fringe work in today's painting, whether it is done by painters or babies or monkeys, is suspect. But your ability to enjoy the wide range of beauty from the old masters to the proven moderns is a sound qualification for directing. It will involve many steps, from such obvious ones as your taste in the colors for your setting and costumes to more complex ones which deal with the succession of pictures you will create with your players on the stage.

In a sense, you face all the problems of the painter for your pictures not only are very large, covering the entire width and height of your setting, but also are in three dimensions, in full color. They change constantly. These changing pictures not only have to be subtly and pleasingly directed but also must enrich, not distract from, the words of the playwright. It may sound difficult. You can enjoy it, however, if you follow the means we will discuss in blocking and if you keep in mind that, as a painter, your materials are human beings in all their amazing possibilities of variety and visual impact. If you've had any hidden self–doubts about your aesthetic broadness because you do not like a "painting" which is six blobs of color apparently thrown at a canvas, cast away the doubts, for your audience, which will be watching raptly when that curtain goes up, wouldn't like such a picture on your stage.

As you begin to catalogue what you like to look at, consider what you like to hear. It is natural for high school ears to revel, depending on their generation, in blues, be–bop, rock, and we have to be patient with that naturalness. But as a director, it is important that you know what you like to hear. I trust that, like your eyes, your ears have developed a fine broad appetite and that you enjoy hearing not only opera and the symphonies but also what musicians call "the standards" and even the best of the "new sounds." This bodes well for what your audience will hear in your play, from the variety and qualities of the voices to whatever music a..d sound effects the production may require.

You thought I might neglect to ask you about voices which please you, but I will not forget, for this is close to the heart of theatre. Am I right, you didn't want to admit that the "full, round tone" seems to you not only unctuous but often insincere and that "English speech" strikes you as affected?

If I've guessed correctly, good for you. In my college days I remember plowing through an awful lot of fol–de–rol about "standard English speech for the stage." And I thought, in my so–green salad days: "This is wrong. This is an American play. We are American actors. We should speak the American language."

In a world in which the American language is becoming the most dominant, British speech does sound affected, no matter which of their hodgepodge of accents and pronunciations is used. Perhaps it eases their pain for having lost the Empire, but the professional Englishmen whom we so generously allow to work in our theatre, our television and our motion pictures, should realize that those affected sounds he makes are beginning to offend American ears. He'll be a better actor and please us if he'll just relax and talk as he hears.

So your fondness for the American language is fortunate for your players and for your audience. Now how do you like it spoken? Naturally, effectively and pleasingly? Very well. In our chapter on Better Speech for Actors we'll take up methods to approach those standards. There may be an extra personal dividend in this discussion for you. The good director needs to communicate clearly, efficiently and sometimes inspirationally with his players. I'm sure it occurs to you that these attributes of speech should be present in the good teacher of any subject and that when they are missing or impaired the best of students is penalized by having to devote precious time and attention to supplying more than his half of the two–way teacher–pupil communication system. Keep in mind that as teacher, and as director, your voice and speech give example, and, since theatre is based upon communicating the words of the playwright, that example should be the best you can make it. You may never be quite as specific as Shakespeare when he said, "Speak the speech, I pray you, as I pronounce it to you," but you often will work very close to his precept.

Our third area of examination is literature. What do you read because you have to, what do you read because you think you should, and what do you read solely because it brings you high pleasure? For a teacher, the answer to the first clause is simple and long: exam papers, the class texts, term papers, related reference works, and on and on. Next the teacher reads scholarly journals, research papers in the field, certain magazines related to the work and, probably, the daily papers. Already, you see, the teacher has done more reading than most other Americans without touching upon the area of reading for pleasure. I know some teachers who get so tired reading the required and the related that they read nothing they enjoy.

This, I'm sure, is not your situation for it is in the third category that we find helpful indications of your potential for directing. I'm hoping that once more we'll find evidence of broad appetite. This is not a place of easy judgment, for many factors insert influence in this matter of reading for pleasure in America. As a teacher you have read more than your share of the fine books, the great books, the enduring books. You don't need to list the courses in high school, college, graduate school that form an imposing monument to your literary experience. Let us hope that the required element did not destroy the real fun and joy and transport inherent in so many masterworks of literature. It may have given you pause occasionally in assigning reading to your own students. From your mature viewpoint you knew the book was fascinating, beautifully written, truly a galleon to carry the reader in ecstacy, but you heard remarks: "I finally finished it. I knew I had to read it." How sad that the "had–to" tag dulls the values for the young mind.

The ground rules stated, let us hear what you read only because it brings you high pleasure. Don't be self–conscious, we're dealing with theatre, and it is man's most human art. You don't belong to a book club? You receive an "A," for book clubs are not for the truly educated. I have nothing against the device in its proper place, and through it at times very excellent books gain wide sale. You see, "sale" is the keystone in the book club structure, not always "literary value." My chief objection is that too many books are read because they are best sellers and that they became best sellers because a committee chose them because they could be sold. I haven't seen research on how many of the acknowledged great books of all time were best sellers in their era of first publication. The publication of Emily Dickinson's work during her lifetime limited her gifts to us to a mere score of poems, not the bountiful one thousand, seven hundred and seventy–five we can now enjoy, even though "The Hidden Life of Emily Dickinson" does question her originality.

We nevertheless are grateful for book clubs, paperbacks and all the other merchandising schemes which have put more books into American hands than ever before in our history. It is good, for it is perhaps better to read anything than not to read at all. Our inquiry, however, is to your reading, and you admit that you avoid the best seller list almost as completely as you avoid book clubs. That seems satisfactory; in some instances, it could be called intelligent. In the arts the mature, educated mind, guided by good taste, rarely needs an imposed buying list. The distance such lists can stray from artistic meaning is shown in the "Top Twenty Records." Of course the book list is far better, for its chief supporters are adults while teen–agers buy the records.

You usually don't read the current "shocking" book? That's commendable not only for time saving but also for taste. Pornography is a very big business in modern life, but, no matter in what form it appears, let us hope that those who know better will not give it support. Do not misunderstand: the subject matter of art is wide, high and low as man's capabilities and culpabilities. The important difference is whether it is art first, then related to dirt, or whether it is first dirt, then perhaps faintly related to art. Dirt sells well, it always has, and its merchants never miss a trick. Sad to say, some current writing for the theatre seems solely in this realm.

Your reading is rather middle of the road, comprised mostly of fiction, occasional mysteries, a few good magazines and once in a while a classic. I feel reluctance in your summarized admission: you read to be entertained. But isn't that what we wanted to know—what you read for pleasure? Oh, you're concerned with semantics. We begin talking about pleasure, in fact the phrase was "high pleasure," and you concluded with "entertainment." Don't feel it unworthy of your academic background. Entertainment is one of the high purposes of theatre. There's one which is more important, but let us give entertainment its full due. This is the rather ephemeral term which makes some people go to the trouble of getting dressed, leaving the cozy routine of television, driving to a playhouse, buying a ticket and sitting down to watch the curtain rise. Most of them come to be entertained, albeit the term means different things to different people. There are central terms which tie audiences together: a well–told story which may bring laughter, tears or excitement, and at times all three; players who live the story, moving and speaking under the rules of good direction; all resulting hopefully in an "evening's entertainment."

Around and above this objective are many others. For the moment, however, consider that the audience, as with you in your reading, is doing something it doesn't have to do. It has, for this night, chosen theatre for entertainment over such formidable rivals as bridge, bowling, television and movies. It will compare, perhaps unconsciously, the value received for its time, trouble and money with the rewards it gets in other areas.

Yes, theatre can inspire, enlighten, elevate and many other noble verbs, but if you don't entertain today's audience it is not apt to come back and give you chances to work your higher magic.

Should you feel any twinge of apology as you contemplate entertaining that future audience, take a quick look at the music and athletic departments of your school. Both fields of endeavor have done such a tremendous job of building themselves securely into the school system, the community and the affections of their audiences that they can have almost anything they ask for. As you watch that beautiful band performing its amazing patterns at the game's half–time, and you recall the thousands of other high school bands, dazzlingly costumed, equipped with the finest instruments and led by excellent conductors, you agree that music truly has a secure and colorful place in the school system. But don't forget what they're doing. Of course they play well, and the teaching of music is the central spine of the whole idea, but the public result is entertainment on a vast and gaudy scale.

So it is with athletics. All the hard work, the training, and the teaching results in entertaining an audience, usually the largest single audience in the community. Athletics and music are the darlings of the public, but they have well earned that affection. Could the theatre begin to please even half those vast audiences there would be little the drama program could not ask for and receive.

The stark truth is that too many high school plays entertain very little, or not at all. Sometimes this is due to inept work on the part of the director and hence by the players. This does not necessarily come from bad intent or laziness but rather from ignorance of everything from play selection to concentration. The result can be frustration for players, director and audience. This is most serious for the third element, since today's public will not willingly seek frustration during leisure hours. In increasing numbers they will stay away from the play and go to hear the band and watch the teams.

Occasionally I meet with teachers who seem to have a positive antipathy toward our word "entertainment." On the chance that you secretly or openly share that viewpoint, let us consider the term a bit more thoroughly. I would guess that these strains of antipathy often emanate from a viewpoint acquired during college years from that egocentric type of professor who grows increasingly smug by downgrading the popular, sometimes in whatever field. It is one thing to stimulate college students properly so that learning becomes an expanding circle of increasing excitement and quite another to tear down and ridicule ordinary standards and beliefs only for the sake of being different. This negative approach to teaching is easiest, I suppose, in the popular arts. What giggles the professor can evoke from his class as he ridicules popular music, popular literature, popular movies, television and theatre! Enough of this and those students leave his class at the end of the year with almost irreparable damage to such essential attributes as tolerance and a broad appetite in considering the arts.

I've known some of these priests of the cult of the high brow, and, among my acquaintances, not one of them was truly a creative person. In some cases, I suspect, they were without talent in the arts. As we so well know, the easiest way for the non–talented to assuage their jealously toward creative people is by ridicule, sarcasm, the bon mot. It is not unlike the performers—"performers" in its narrowest sense, the sense which would include trained seals—who actually are paid money on television and in night clubs to do sarcastic, exaggerated and often cruel imitations of famous stars. The laughter they drag from the non–talented also has a tinge of satisfied jealousy: "Huh, that star's no better than me. See how silly he looks when he's imitated by an impressionist."

From this sometimes frightening background of abasement we find many people with long academic backgrounds who have been so upset with the popular that they tend also to negate the entertaining. In our consideration of secondary school play production, this is a serious matter, a matter in which we must obtain true clarity of terms. This urgency stems from case after case of teachers who have chosen plays far beyond the capabilities of both the students and their audience for but one reason, this ingrown fear that the popular would soil by contact and that entertainment has no academic validity. I've tried to explain to some of these misguided that the band could, with practice, play Bartok between halves of the homecoming game but that Rogers and Hammerstein were better for the occasion and the audience.

Upon one occasion I had the all–revealing answer: "I had a professor at the University who taught us that nothing which entertains has true artistic merit!" Let us hope that the meaning lost something in translation and that what the man said was, "Great popularity may lessen artistic stature." He could prove this point rather quickly by reading us the list of the five most popular television programs, but if the man is fair and honest he cannot insist that entertainment and artistic merit are incompatible.

Let us note some of the meanings Webster gives to "entertain": "To receive into or keep in the mind, to consider or dwell upon." The dictionary also says, "to engage the attention of, agreeably."

Didn't these things happen to you when you recently heard music you liked, read a book you enjoyed, saw a play which brought you pleasure? Of course they did; you were entertained. The artistic quality of the material may be limited by the mind concerned or by the attention engaged, but both mind and attention can gain in facility with time and experience. There is little chance for an audience to gain facility if we bore them out of the theatre.

The night when you will have an audience as guests at your play lies ahead. For the sake of other plays you may do and of all living theatre, you will not want the experience to drive it away with boredom but rather you should hope to engage its attention agreeably so that it will receive in its minds and consider the story of your play; so that you may entertain it. If this entertainment can compete with the blandishments offered by all the other leisure–time activities available, your audience may be well disposed for a return visit to your next play and other plays.

What theatre have you seen which made you want more theatre? This answer may take time, but we trust it will include such items as the road companies which presented some of the greatest talent of our stage. A visit to Broadway would make certain your delight in this kind of theatre. Perhaps you have found real satisfaction in community theatre productions where the play often makes a more complete impact than is possible when the audience pays first attention to one or two stars in the cast. Your list may also quite properly include several college productions, for this is the kind of theatre which is best housed today and on many campuses is well taught. I hope your pleasurable experience includes at least one high school production and that you can recall what you liked about it.

Much can be learned about direction by observation, not only of well–directed plays but also by careful scrutiny and evaluation of those which are badly directed. At first you may find this difficult for the effective production tends to catch you up in the experience and your involvement tends to cloud the analytic process. This is as it should be and illustrates the empathic power of good living theatre. It is true for me, and I have had the extreme privilege of directing two hundred and eighty major productions. You may want to follow my procedure for learning by observation. The best way is to see the production again and watch the means by which the director and his players weave their spell. Second viewing is often not practical so we then recall the play in sequence and see if we can separate cause from effect.

In your initial attempts you may find your study resulting chiefly in generalities: the play was easy to hear; it was pleasant to watch; it held your interest consistently; the high emotional points affected you. You may think these points too simple, but they hold the simplicity inherent in true art. The ways to them depend greatly on fundamentals. One of the obvious differences between the "arty" and the artistic is that the former usually ignores fundamentals and gets lost in nebulous theories holding no real values. As one who has followed football with pleasure from the days of Knute Rockne to Vince Lombardi and Tom Landry, I have found that the great winning coaches are those who best taught the importance of perfect execution of fundamentals which, in the case of football, start with blocking and tackling.

We're going to discuss the ways in which you can make your play easy to hear and pleasant to watch. We will see if we can make it hold interest consistently and give the emotional peaks their proper values. But develop your observation ability with every play you see; it will teach you more and more. A young man named Herb Gardner used the method to become a playwright. For several years he worked in Broadway theatres selling refreshments between the acts or checking wraps. Each performance he studied the play and, after a few weeks, managed to get assignment to another theatre where he had new subject matter. It worked for Herb Gardner; his "A Thousand Clowns" won success amidst the rugged competition of the New York theatre.

A pleasant truth for those who would direct is that much of the observation of your entire life can be useful, once you have learned the ability to recall and the technique of translating real–life elements to the needs of your players and your play.

To transpose an immortal line, "The stage can be all the world."

chapter three

EXPLORING THE STUDENT POTENTIAL

Athletic and music scholarships have become so firmly a part of our college system that it would be a rash fellow indeed who would ever question their complete propriety. On most campuses they seem to return full value for the money in building reputation, adding color to university life and entertaining the public which pays most of the total bills for the institution. It has become quite an industry. Recently a university announced it was considering giving up conference competition because the coaching staff did not believe they could field proper teams with only ninety athletic scholarships available.

That is all very well, but I happen to know that in the same school the important drama department felt most fortunate to have five graduate assistantships. A fair balance? Perhaps, since theatre is a late comer to education, and has neglected woefully logical steps to build itself into the essential university structure.

The secondary school, however, is our prime concern. Here

we have coaches and teachers of music working successfully without benefit of subsidized talent. I venture that music could have succeeded with little more than the long–established American precept: "Every child should take music lessons." The high school athletic program stands on an equally firm foundation, the components of which are such activities for grade school children as Little Leagues, playground activities and some team play, and in the junior high years, physical education courses and highly organized team activities.

You see my point: your colleagues on the faculty are moving toward their music and athletic performances with material which has been exposed to the principles and practice of their respective subjects for almost the entire school life of the child. You, however, presently will announce tryouts for a play and may have to execute your intricate assignment with material untrained in any aspect of living theatre.

Happily this is not the total situation. Those of you who fortunately teach speech classes to sophomores, or even juniors, have a potential place of discovery and training. If there is also a dramatic club your tools are doubled, and it is up to you to find and prepare those with talent for theatre.

You'll see that last phrase rarely mentioned in writings about secondary school dramatic activities. There is a peculiar reticence among educators regarding talent for theatre, although they long have acclaimed the existence of such things as "talent for music," "talent for sports," "talent for language," "talent for math," "talent for painting," and even such a strange occupant of the educational bed as "talent for cooking."

Part of the reason for this persistent blind spot is that nearly all other "talents" involve solo performances, whereas an actor, to perform, must be part of an ensemble. Even in a team sport, the coaches can quite fully evaluate each player long before the first scheduled game; this is not as easy with actors.

When you begin to cast your play, you are going to have to judge talent quickly and your judgment will determine much of the final result. Is it not then logical to try to evaluate the material to some extent before the fateful moment of casting arrives?

If you have the speech or drama class and/or the dramatic club, this work is much easier because you have an established time period in which to pursue it. Without such a time period, you may have to observe pupils in your own classes which may be in subjects far removed from theatre. This method is not completely hopeless because you can observe your students talking, responding, reacting: some of the stuffs from which theatre is made.

A priceless ingredient in theatre is personality projection; it is in fact one of the chief factors in the making of a motion picture star. If this personality projection includes the rarer element of great charm, we have actors like Gary Cooper or Clark Gable. In their long and illustrious careers both men were quick to admit that many were better actors, yet they held the spark which a star must have.

You are not looking for stars as you begin to survey your material, but the youngster whose personality comes through clearly and strongly may well be a potential player. The introvert, the dark, moody child, is not so apt to illumine a stage, though I'm sure there are exceptions. The extreme extrovert, the show–off, likewise is unlikely stage material. I have found it true with adults. When I am told of a drawing room comedian whose friends say he ought to be on the stage, I know that the stage is one place he should never be.

Acting is not for the flip, the arrogant, the brash; it needs kinder and warmer qualities. The ordinary citizen is too well fooled by actors; he confuses the performance with the man or the woman. It would be hard to find two gentler, more reticent men than Boris Karloff and Peter Lorre, yet they could act the monsters and the villains. It is said that the most sober luncheon in California occurs when Jack Benny, George Burns, Groucho Marx and perhaps Joey Bishop are gathered around a table. These men are not funny in the living room; they use their talent for comedy in performances.

You may dismiss the smart aleck of the class as unlikely material for the stage, and continue your search for deeper and more valued attributes. Sincere enthusiasm is a sound virtue and found, I believe, in most of the important theatre folk. An actor without sincerity or an actor without enthusiasm would be difficult to use in a play. Enthusiasm has a double function on the stage, giving first of all to the individual a zest for the long hard road of rehearsal. Later, sincere enthusiasm tends to show through in performance.

I feel this quality is most significant when it permeates his entire viewpoint of life. A student who has no enthusiasm for school itself, perhaps to the point of failing a subject or two, has not the best possibilities as an actor. You see, theatre should not be used as a refuge from reality, a crutch for a disturbed ego, or as therapy for the despondent. The privilege of being in a play and the joys which come with a successful production bring many dividends to the participants, but that is not the real objective. They are only part of the reward which the living theatre gives to those who are its good practitioners.

I once read some ridiculous nonsense about how the theatre experience could well be used for moral and physical cures: make the bad boy better by letting him play the virtuous hero and so on and so on and so on. This is heresy to all the verities of living theatre. Don't let anyone ever impose any such approach to casting on you.

Margaret and I have used scores of high school students in our productions over the years, and we have found several continuing truths. The young people invariably are superior, always as human beings and nearly always as students. At the time of casting we make it understood that the privilege of being in a community theatre production increases, rather than lessens, the obligation to all phases of school work. We explain that the old chestnut is true: "Busy people are the ones who get things done." Five night rehearsals a week means that their study time must be completely and efficiently organized.

They soon understand this and usually begin to expand the limits of their work range. As I said, they are superior human beings or they never would have had the energy and courage to try for parts or crew work at a community playhouse. This superiority, aided by our teaching approach, has resulted in the Youngs' happy report that in thirty years of using high school students they have simultaneously met their full school obligations. A great majority, according to pleased parents and teachers, have raised their grade averages during the period of rehearsal and performance.

You should be gratified and not necessarily surprised if you find the greatest interest in your forthcoming dramatic work among the best students, the leaders who are present in every classroom. We can project a correlation between acting qualities and success in adult life. Aren't the most famous doctors and lawyers those who seem well cast in their real–life roles? Who could "play" great generals better than MacArthur, Eisenhower and LeMay? A fine waiter, service station man or salesman seems to have sincere enthusiasm, an essential enjoyment of his duties which makes them a pleasure for him and for you.

Although all actors can't be of triple–A grade, anymore than practitioners of other activities, the inferior person is apt to find little in theatre to his liking. The work is too hard and the discipline too strong for the lazy, the incompetent or the malcontented. Among other lacks, the inferior student probably is short on imagination, an important ingredient for an actor. Secondary school tends to stifle the display of imagination so the teacher needs to take extra care in discovering and nurturing this fragile attribute of the human mechanism. These are the years when your students live under tremendous pressure to conform, to keep in step with the mass, to heed such vital observances of the group code as the proper color of socks for school wear, when to learn, likewise forget, a certain dance step.

Evidence of imagination comes to you in many ways. It appears in what students write for you, in what they say to you, and in the responses they make to what you say. This tendency to submerge imagination in high school is in complete contrast to the younger child who, in his "let's play like" years, lives very close to some of the basic factors of living theatre. Could we but develop the beautiful freedom of expression and exultant imagination of the small child with continuous theatre training straight through high school what wonders we might achieve! It would be very similar to the music lessons continuing until the student enters the high school band.

That state hopefully belongs to a later day and, at the moment, you need more devices to discover the material for your play. Those of you who have a class in speech or drama thereby hold the mechanics for talent discovery. With such a class you are well ahead because most of the students, if it is an elective, are apt to be of the superior group. There may be exceptions for sometimes the lazy or incompetent think a course in the arts is "easy." In the broad sense this is an obvious fallacy for, given teachers of equal competence, which student has the "easiest" labor: he who learns to work a problem in math or he who learns to write a sonnet? Is it easier to learn to do an experiment in chemistry or to play a role expertly and satisfactorily?

You have a wide range of methods available in your search for talent. Improvisations are a good starting point and should be begun early in the first semester. This involves setting premises; you can devise the initial ones and the students, who will enjoy the experience, may begin to offer subsequent ones. The story can be simple, perhaps using some of actual situations from high school life. You then cast the play and discuss the characters. Let two or three of the less positive students arrange the furniture for the scene. There will be a good bit of shyness at first but participation of any kind eases tension. Let the improvisations run as long as they make progress, and don't be disappointed if they are quite short in the beginning. If you set one day a week for this exercise you doubtless will find that soon the quality of the performances and the stories themselves will grow until the improvisations are the high point of the week.

Here are some suggested story lines. Allow the students three minutes to set the general plan to be followed. To allow for reasonable development, the time range should be between ten and fifteen minutes.

1. A boy decides it is his duty to enlist in the Peace Corps. Two friends of his try to dissuade him. The decision depends on the strongest arguments.

2. A boy and a girl meet with the music chairman for the school dance. One wants a group of folk singers to furnish the music, and the other wants an orchestra hired which will play dance music.

3. Three people survive a plane crash and reach a desert island. Each wants to establish his favorite form of government.

4. Two girls are left alone one night in a lonely summer cottage on the lake. They hear mysterious noises outside and work out a course of action. Of course the telephone isn't working!

5. Three good friends work together in an office. A representative of a national firm comes to tell one of them that he, or she, has won a contest prize of a trip to Europe for two. The winner has to decide which of his two friends he will take to Europe.

6. A foreign exchange student has arrived at school and on the first day meets with two or three classmates to find out how to act to be a success in an American school.

7. A student goes for an interview about a summer job with an office manager or storeowner. The competition is very keen for the position.

8. Two young actors in New York meet in a drug store after not seeing each other for a year. Each is afraid to tell the other that he or she has landed a part in a new show for fear of discouraging the other who has had no work. The happy climax comes when they discover that they have both been hired for the same production.

If time permits you may be able to move into improvisations with larger groups. Here are a few suggested story lines.

1. A family of six or eight has a reunion at a back yard barbecue. Most of the brothers, sisters, cousins, aunts and uncles have not seen each other for two or three years. Everything is pleasant until old quarrels are renewed.

2. Workers on an assembly line are about to strike when word is brought that one–half their demands will be met. Their acceptance or rejection of the terms and their course of action provides good opportunity for the actors.

3. A group of politicians tries to persuade a candidate to give up his race for the nomination and support his rival.

4. A group of tourists to the World's Fair decides they will tell the guide what they want to see. They organize the tour the way they want it and then go on with the sightseeing.

5. A group of scientists at Cape Kennedy prepares for the launching of the last manned flight to the moon. The countdown finishes, and what happens?

If your people gain some facility you may want to let the larger group exercises run up to twenty minutes. The length is not as important as the time in which they are effective.

Some questions which you may ask after the work is moving along are these:

1. Does the conversation flow freely?

2. Is the story acted clearly and at reasonable speed or is it hurried through superficially?

3. Are the characterizations fairly clear?

4. Do the thought patterns seem honest?

5. Are the emotions genuine?

The material for improvisation is almost as plentiful as life itself. If the students get caught up in the project they can begin to supply ideas from such sources as the daily papers, magazines, and scenes from the plots of novels, biographies and short stories. The actual history of your town and region is likely to provide usable material.

This beginning course of action can be managed rather easily by those of you with classes in speech or drama but what of you who are without such a ready–made work arena? My suggestion is to form a dramatic club, an organization which certainly belongs in any high school which produces one or more plays a year. I believe school authorities will be cooperative once you explain that the club is needed to reach those not enrolled in your classes. These might appear when you finally announce tryouts for the play, but how much better if you can get to know most of them and begin to appraise their abilities before you get to casting.

The next step in what we might call the discovery and development phase of your procedure is to have students work on scenes from plays. This gives a new dimension to the theatre experience and logically follows the exercises in improvisation. Your people no longer must create dialogue; it is written for them by experts, the playwrights. Scene work can be a highly stimulating experience for both students and teacher and is a move closer to the final function of the actor.

There has been a drastic shortage for years of carefully selected and edited scenes for this highly important endeavor. In my writing in the area of theatre, I have tried always to serve where there is need. More than a hundred published articles will, I think, attest to my sincerity. In response to the need of teachers and actors for scene material, I wrote my fourth book. *Audition Scenes for Students* contains twenty–four scenes for one actor, one actress and combinations up to five actors.

The playwrights of *Audition Scenes for Students* range from Aeschylus and Plautus, Shakespeare and Rostand, to an interesting variety of contemporary authors. To make this actor's tool more effective I have written sections on "Memorization," "Variety in Line Reading," "Listening," "Concentration" and "Characterization."

The final phase of exploratory work in class or club, or both, should encompass learning lines and rehearsing. This phase can be contracted or expanded as fits your time and energy and the student–power available. If you have a large and talented group you can cast several one–acts and set performance dates for the class or the club. Should one play give evidence of really being finished, you no doubt can get it scheduled for an assembly appearance before the entire student body. Be certain, however, that it will please. You can judge this by the club's reaction. Then make sure it is done well enough to build goodwill for the whole idea of high school drama. Success with a one–act at assembly can be of real help in selling the major production when it comes along. The assembly performance may require royalty payment so be sure to check with the publishers before you plan to produce it. Classroom work on plays usually is permitted without fee.

If you are able to pursue these avenues for exploration of the student potential you will approach tryout time for the major production far better prepared. You will have learned much about the students with an interest in theatre, and they will have begun to learn some of the techniques of the actor. While the journey is long, you have begun and now are ready, much more ready than you were, to select the play.

chapter four

HOW TO SELECT A PLAY

Play selection is a continuing problem in theatre, a problem as obtuse and exasperating now as it was twenty–five centuries ago when a handful of Greeks tried to decide which of the submitted manuscripts should be produced to compete for the prize. It is perhaps most formidable today in the producing center with the world's greatest collection of experts, Broadway. Here the question has the grimmest of undertones for, if the choice is wrong, vast sums of money are lost and scores of actors and technicians return to their state of unemployment. The people who make the decisions for Broadway have great talent and usually long experience. Yet, season after season, the ratio of failure to success continues about seven to three.

There are touching attempts to lower this failure average from seventy per cent, a common one being to copy a hit which uses new subject matter. This rarely succeeds, the plays which follow the hit, although they are written about the same subject and have casts, directors, designers and producers of equal skill, do not often catch the scent of the sweet smell of success. This seems a difficulty peculiar to theatre for, in most other arts, imitation often pays its way. The painter and the composer often can coast prosperously on the coattails of trend or a style.

This lazy philosophy, "How to Succeed by Merely Copying," is flagrantly present with one of our mechanical colleagues, television. A producer who has seen his sponsors disappear when he tried a new idea knows that he soon can entice them back if he'll turn out shows about cowboys, doctors, private investigators or any other current favorite of the rating services. Such thinking has not speeded television's growth into maturity, as any consistent viewer can tell you almost as quickly as he can list the fine programs which once were on the air. This is perhaps but one more of the basic differences between the telecast and the living theatre. The French might say, "Viva la difference!"

You are saying that you don't have to please those several men who pronounce critical judgment on the work of Broadway or the sponsors who pay the way for television. Quite true, but you have some people and some purposes to please. In their own way, they will keep you quite busy in the doing.

First, the people, and at the head of that list is your audience. We agree that until the prepared play and the audience meet in mutual experience living theatre, per se, does not truly exist. I once heard a self–adoring director say he didn't care if anyone came to see his plays. Feeling very secure under the umbrella of a foundation grant for his stock–company type operation, he proceeded to do plays with which his potential audiences could make no contact. They stayed away in larger and larger numbers until there were none. Then one day the grant ran out. End of story.

Do not, on the other hand, take television's experience as law. There were some audiences for *Playhouse 90, Matinee Theatre, Alcoa Playhouse,* the *Richard Boone Theatre* and other well–conceived and splendidly executed drama series, but the rating systems insist upon a majority of the available audience as the only criterion of success. You work under no such unbearable standard. Many will come to your play because of relationship to and interest in the students involved and because of enthusiasm for the entire activity program of the high school. For others in the community, who enjoy, or might enjoy, living theatre, the factor of giving satisfaction becomes important. The more of these that can be drawn into a continuing audience, the more certain it is that the program can not only survive but can, with time, grow in importance and quality.

It is the interest level and taste of this fringe audience which should not be under—or over—estimated. Frankly, they may enthuse over a higher entertainment possibility than that offered by an endless wagon train of cowboys and Indians, but they probably would not show up for very many in a series of Ibsen plays. That can't be managed even with the rich resources of Broadway. The rational path to finding a play lies in the middle ground of quality drama.

The second group of individuals you will want to please are the school authorities, the administration of the school itself and the echelon above, normally the school board. I place them in second place for if we fail to please and keep an audience, the drama program will disintegrate and vanish. I have known sincere teachers who have worked very hard to produce high school plays of quality but who forgot to please the administration. In some cases they did works which startled or shocked or which were opposed to the mores of the town. This also can be fatal. Part of the overall contact living theatre ought to make is fitting into the tastes and moral standards of its potential audience. If it violates these standards the results are disturbance of the viewers and, in the case of noncommercial productions, usually resentment which may bring about drastic action.

There is nothing courageous in using living theatre for protest or pornography. The stage is not a speakers' platform nor should it be a place to sell junk. The New York theatre, like a drowning man, has been grasping at any straw. It thought tickets could be sold if the new show out–shocked the previous top–shocker. But there is a diminishing market for filth. The small list of the Anglo–Saxons' four–letter words becomes dull with repetition and finally loses all interest except to the permanently retarded who are really little boys scrawling dirty words on the alley fence.

After *Oh, Calcutta,* where was there to go in that direction? Another naked show proves only how unappetizing most people are with their clothes off in public. The age–old aesthetic law has not been repealed; sensual aesthetic pleasure always has come from the mystery of semiconcealment. The continuing diminution of On and Off–Broadways' audiences is due in part to the distressing image of New York as a city and to the lessening proportion of out–of–towners who once swelled those audiences. They began to return to Dubuque and Albuquerque feeling that New York plays were too violently removed from the moral precepts of their normal lives.

A sensible course is to avoid displeasing the high school administration. Get your play approved well ahead of announcement time. If the principal likes the text you are going to produce, you are building important good will for your entire program. He and the school board are held responsible for the conduct and the image of the entire school. They must see that the play you present will not offend the tastes and mores of the community. One or two brave souls among you may be quick to say, "My principal knows nothing about theatre. Why should he have anything to do with selecting my play?"

Please restrain your emotions while you listen again; we are not asking anyone to help you choose a play but rather are making a safety check at the proper point so you will not endanger your work or your program by doing the wrong play. Remember that school administrators represent community viewpoints also. If you displease them you may well displease large segments of the audience. Occasionally directors in high school, university or community theatre produce plays which shock or offend and the results often are disastrous. On one occasion the entire drama staff of thirteen left a university after a play was stopped in mid–run by the president. It was a great play by a great American playwright, but it was the wrong play for that campus theatre.

Most community theatres use the protective screen of a play reading committee to avoid such dangers, but headstrong directors sometimes go wrong even with this safeguard. The device is hard to use in a high school situation. Bringing in the administration in any way to participation and interest in the drama is a wise move. Getting its reaction to a proposed manuscript has a potential for good.

The third group of people to please are the students who will be working on the production. This is not difficult because if your play seems likely to please an audience and if it has been approved by the administration the attitude of the students should reflect your own reaction. As a teacher you build enthusiasms almost daily for subject matter of a book, an idea, a project; the play needs the same stimulation of morale.

Are you ahead of me? Have you guessed the one other person who must be pleased by the play? It is you. Although creative work cannot be done at its best unless the artist is happy with the material, often in high school theatre we go wrong at this very point. Many times through the years I have been startled when a teacher friend has said: "Oh, I'm doing this (naming a play) but I'm not sure I like it."

Stop at this brink and fully note the danger. You would neither expect an artist to paint his best into a picture he disliked nor a musician to play with any joy a composition he couldn't stand. But I fear many plays appear on high school stages disliked by their directors. The result? Less, often much less, than it should be. A director should be emotionally involved with the manuscript. He should have affection, admiration, excitement, belief and, in rare instances, all of these for it. In its best sense, directing is a translation and projection of his viewpoint to his stage. Occasionally I find inspiration in a manuscript, and then I try very hard to translate that rare emotion to the production.

The reverse of the coin is obvious. Disinterest, disdain, dislike of the play by the director may appear all over the stage when that curtain parts. This is the very center of the problem. What happens to you when you read a play, or see a play, is terribly important. If the reactions are those so essential to good work you have a positive, not a negative, point of departure for your production.

Perhaps you read few plays and find it difficult to get definite impressions from the printed page. The way to improvement is by reading. Thus far in history no mind has appeared which has been able to say of an unproduced manuscript, "This will be a success." Your reading, I think, ought to be in accumulating proven works, those purified by the agonies of production so that the rewriting, the changing, the elimination and addition have resulted in something that works with an audience when well–produced. Read within limits, but within those boundaries read widely: the good, the bad, the indifferent. It's surprising how much you can learn of what makes a good play by reading a number of poor ones.

Seeing performances is an easier way of evaluation, but it also holds problems. If you are thrilled by a great star in a play, take a second look and be certain that the play will stand up without the virtuoso talent. A strong point of community theatre, as we have pointed out, is that the play itself often gets a more rounded projection than the same work performed under the commercial star system. Through the years high schools of our region often have done plays seen by the teachers at the Shreveport Little Theatre. The performances made the play seem attractive enough to use in the high school program.

The first time you read an unfamiliar play don't be concerned with such technical details as the size and proportion of the cast, the number of settings, unusual demands for costumes or properties. Read for story value and emotional experience. These are the items of real value. Unless the story interests and moves you, there is little chance you can make it a worthwhile experience for your audience. The degree to which you can visualize the words you read as a performance will depend upon your imagination and your experience in playreading. Both can be developed by time and industry.

Suppose that of ten plays you read three have stories you like. You have found them amusing or exciting or touching or any combination of strong emotional values. Now is the time to read again, considering the mechanical and technical possibilities. If one calls for three or four elaborate settings and expensive costumes, you perhaps should save it for a day when you have gained the technical facilities to handle such a production. Of the remaining two, each may call for a single set and modern dress; in short, there may be no important mechanical difference between the two manuscripts.

Now it is well to think of the students with whom you have been working. Although you may expect others to appear at the tryouts, it is not likely the ability of the unknowns will exceed greatly what you already have found in the others. Do not try to pre–cast at this point. A director ought to begin tryouts with an open mind, because delightful surprises in talent may appear out of nowhere. Your problem is to loosely evaluate the general ability of the students you have come to know and to see if you can imagine them meeting the demands of these plays you like. An extreme example of this point would be the teacher considering "Hamlet." Not often would a high school boy seem remotely possible in this role, and yet some Shakespeare can be managed. In Shreveport we have had excellent high school productions of "Taming of the Shrew," "Twelfth Night," and even "The Merchant of Venice," but I have to admit that the director was a man of fine talent and long experience, with a special gift for Shakespearean production.

You may find this judging of capabilities difficult at first. It is more prudent to underestimate than to overestimate your students. This standard practice in athletics explains not only the classification of high school teams but also, at the college level, gives good reason for Slippery Rock not scheduling a football game with Nebraska University.

You'll learn to do this better in time, but let us assume you feel both your plays are possible with the material you have. There is one difference between the two; the first is quoted as "ten dollars royalty" while the second has a price tag of "twenty–five." The principal may find both plays suitable for school production and suggest you use the ten dollar item to "save" fifteen dollars before you start.

Perhaps the general public will never understand this matter of royalty. Men and women who admit happily the validity of prices on nearly every item in American life and who are apt to say, with an air of profundity, "You get what you pay for," are the very ones who think royalty a rather silly matter to begin with and always select the lesser figure.

Years ago I wrote, "Royalty is the best money you spend in connection with play production." I stand by the truth of the statement with more determination each year. If there is a single factor which predetermines the value of the end result in living theatre, it is the quality of the manuscript. Thirty or forty times a year this is proven in New York. The most expert talents in the American theatre, with vast sums of money to implement their efforts, work prodigiously, and come up with failures, because, in the critics' consensus "the play was weak, shoddy, unrealized" or occasionally the reviews shorten it to "no good."

It behooves us in the noncommercial theatre, where money is always in short supply and much of our talent is latent or undeveloped, to put the best possible foundation under our work, namely the best available text. With that anchor to windward, the chances of success are considerable. Without it, they are almost negligible.

Of course there are exceptions to the infallibility of the royalty price tag; some ten–dollar plays are better than some which cost fifty or twenty–five dollars for the first performance. The chances, however, of stumbling on such a hidden prize are remote indeed. It is likewise true that many plays of the higher figure are not worth doing, but the general quality of these scripts is much higher.

If there is any difficulty with the administration over the amount to be spent on royalty, you should learn it early and take steps to overcome the problem. You might use the argument that the coaches would not permit their boys to go into team play without the best of equipment, nor would the band want to use inferior instruments. You might add that even in such dire cases the results could be better than trying to produce an inferior play. The team still might win the game, and the band still might play successfully by compensating for its poor instruments, but when your work was finished you still would be exhibiting an inferior play.

This matter is so important that, should a crisis develop, it would be intelligent to save expenses in another direction rather than skimp on royalty. Better to have a good text played on a bare stage than a poor one dressed in a thousand dollars worth of settings and costumes. Most school administrators are reasonable people and will understand, if you explain it well, that a production is limited in potential by the printed text from which it is made and that whatever the present goal, it will be more nearly reached if you buy quality material with payment of top royalty.

chapter five

CASTING A PLAY

Choosing the play is a big decision, but selecting the players for specific roles is perhaps even more monumental. To decide which of the young people, all probably equally inexperienced, can in a few brief weeks of rehearsal give capable performances is difficult indeed. To augment the stress, casting decisions should be made only by the director.

The director–actor relationship is most intricate, involving not only a teacher–pupil position but also the artist's kinship with his material, the guide and his strength to induce exact following, the disciplinarian and his ability to give discipline pleasant overtones, and the inspirational leader who often can make human beings exceed their best.

Such demands make the director's position more difficult than that of the conductor of music who works in some of the same areas but with a fundamental and vital difference: in theatre the actor is his own instrument. In the band it matters not whether a trumpet player is five or six–feet tall, whether he be ugly or handsome. The quality of his voice and the precision of his speech are of no moment. Be his personality radiant or dourly submerged, it matters not because most of the human being is hidden under that gorgeous uniform with horn in front. The dominant, almost the only, question for the conductor is: "How well does he play the trumpet?"

Would that living theatre asked no more from its central guiding force. Each of the relationships mentioned, and there are more, break down into a whole series of contributive, but essential, points. Considering only the teacher–pupil consanguinity which is a daily reality for those involved in the high school play, it affects not only your students but also the others who may come to tryouts. There will be, or should be, one difference: this is work which the young person does not have to do, no law requires his presence in the play, and you have no imminent grade–card club to hold over his head. With these strengths of the classroom situation removed, the director faces a vast teaching assignment, which must be done rapidly and exactly. To succeed it needs a special mental adrenalin which you can help instill, the desire to please you and a will for success.

This same fragile but constant predominance of the personal, in all its multitudinous variations, is present in other areas of the director–actor situation. The artist viewing his material—in your case a group of young people with whom, and out of whom, you have to create a performance—has to feel confidence and belief. Confidence will vary, and at times you may feel that *any* other group of students might do better, but relax, this is part of the splendid tribulation of making theatre.

To find a successful path through this maze of interpersonal relationships the director must have sole authority in casting. In some ways this is more important than your feeling about the play itself. You might succeed with a work which a committee had chosen if it were a sound play. The necessary enthusiasm could develop with study, and rehearsal could begin in some comfort. It is far less likely that good working conditions could emerge if the director were handed a cast chosen by others, either an individual or committee. Unlike printed pages which can't fight back as you work on them, human beings assigned by others probably never would achieve the best working relationship with the director. The fault is double–edged; the director's recurring thought is that if he'd chosen the players there would be important changes; the students may wonder why they should play well on the team of one who didn't choose them.

The casting committee almost has disappeared from even the darkest corners of the American theatre but, if you ever have a chance to complete the eradication, please do your part. Such an aesthetically immoral device only could have happened because of a soft point in theatre's structure: well–done plays look so easy to the layman that he thinks he could do any part of them if he cared to be so generous.

The same citizen will sit quietly subdued at a performance by his civic symphony or the local opera group and never venture to say, "I could compose a concerto as good as that" or, "Give me some paper and a pencil and I'll write you a better opera than that!" Yet let him view a play he doesn't care for, done by his fellow townsmen, and he will proclaim, "I could write a better play than that," or, "I could act better than that with my hands tied behind my back."

This citizen is a bit in awe of music because "you have to take lessons to learn that stuff" and the hieroglyphics of musical scores keep him at a distance, but living theatre appears deceptively easy. This talkative friend never would presume to take over functions of television or motion pictures. These, as he would say, are "industries," and that's stable. Both are made by machines and, in his words, "You can't fool around with machines; you got to know how to run 'em."

Small wonder that the stage is subject to pronouncements by the uninformed; it is not an industry, it is not made by machines, and we don't do much about "taking lessons to learn that stuff." But herein may lie part of the reason for living theatre's puzzling endurance: most Americans are practicing actors and playwrights in their own minute way. To inform yourself on this point, observe the world around you for the next two days. Listen particularly to the performances people give when they quote someone else. Nearly always the scene is overdone in voice, gesture and facial expression. Here is the citizen as actor, normally beginning with "And he said . . ." or "Then she said . . ." In this phase of human conduct, even the kindest of souls tends to give the extra edge to the quoted voice, the exaggeration of face and gesture, which results in vocal and visual satire. This happens not only when the roles played are those of enemies but also with the portraits of friends.

The same acid approach appears in the ad–lib playwriting which you hear every day, those little gems built around an incident, often of no interest to the cornered listener, but selected by the storyteller because his is a starring role. The subject matter is unimportant and often deadly dull, such as the argument with the checker at the supermarket. It is the role which is vital, the role written as the speaker starts, "So I said" and continues "And then he said . . ." and on and on and on. As the story builds, the teller has the aesthetic privilege of playing lines as he writes them, and acting both sides of the scene. I have yet to hear one of these self–written, self–acted treasures in which the talker did not come out best, nor one in which the opponent was not satirized almost unmercifully. No wonder the Show Biz "impressionists" get such applause when they crucify famous people. This is the kind of acting the folks understand; they do it themselves every day!

This tenuous bond between citizen and stage partially may explain why the Fabulous Invalid has survived for twenty–five centuries; it is Man's most human art. Its very nearness to life provides countless difficulties for its practitioners. The transmutation of the continual, everyday experience of human beings talking, listening, reacting into an aesthetic experience worth the cost of a ticket is subtle, demanding and difficult.

Much depends on the choice of material in most arts. Canvas, marble, paper, and pigments, to name but a few, are more quickly definable than players reading lines for a director. Your colleagues of film and tape, for whom the visual aspect comes first, have an easier time. Almost any beauty queen (and did you know that we choose about three thousand each year in the fifty states) can be made to say the line right for one "take" that is "printed." The bit of film or tape then is pasted to the growing reel in the can and, when each item in the script has been done right once and photographed, the director's task is done, unless he does his own editing.

Not so on stage, for here the role must be mastered as a whole and done correctly not just once but repeated correctly through final rehearsals, all performances. It is important to seek the proper quality for the role first. Later, physical qualifications may be considered. The quality you seek should match your feeling about each character. Your reaction need not match that of the director who did the commercial production. He may have had to subvert many points to the star system.

The descriptive paragraphs in front of playbooks are not much help. Example: "Suzy is twenty–nine, short and red–headed and talks like a machine gun. Basically she is a kind and sensitive person." You may pretty much ignore the first sentence but must pay attention to the second, for it treats of quality. Age and hair coloring are mechanical matters. In high school we achieve age with makeup, and today's plethora of wigs provides a director with instant hair change. Of course a director of brief experience should not stray far from the playwright's basic demands and purposes, but consideration of your own concepts often can pay dividends.

All possible participants should be encouraged to attend tryouts. In addition to the time and place, spread word of the exciting, pleasurable elements of the play. If you cannot achieve the impact attendant to the announcement of the call for aspirants to the football squad at least work in that direction.

Keep the playbooks away from the students. Actors of any age are notoriously bad at casting themselves. It is a serious handicap to have players coming to tryouts with preconceived notions about the parts they want. If you let it happen, those who have miscast themselves are likely to be unhappy when you want to put them in the roles to which they are suited. A wise actor knows that the greatest kindness a director can show is to cast him properly, but that wisdom usually comes with years.

Begin tryouts by having the group fill out three–by–five cards listing name, age and any acting experience, which may go back to grade school or children's theatre. Leave the lower half of the cards blank for your notes on their reading. They keep the cards until it is their turn.

Discuss the playwright and the play briefly, but don't tell the story. Let the impact of that come from the reading. Explain that you are not looking for performances but rather impressions. If possible, let each read more than once and perhaps in more than one role. The timetable is explained: there will be individual call–backs for the most suitable and then a group–reading in a week using the best candidates, then more call–backs and a final group reading at the end of two weeks at which time you should be ready for decisions.

Knowing they are not on immediate and final trial relaxes students. With your guidance they should enjoy the play as it is read. You may have guessed the second reason for not passing out playbooks before a first tryout. Theatre is first an *aural* experience, as you know, and plays come to us best for the first time through our ears. Change the readers every four or five minutes so that you may have second readings from most. These second rounds often bring surprises. The student who sounded hopeless the first time, having found the experience wasn't fatal, may read a sentence, or even a phrase, which sounds like the character. This is the nugget of quality you seek; note the find on the card for further exploration.

If the tryout gets to the middle of the second act, go back to the beginning of the play and re–read. Naturally the group now will be eager to learn what happens next, a sound psychological step in building interest in the play itself. When the Youngs do a mystery play, we always Scotchtape the third act shut before tryouts and keep it sealed until the third group reading. We often keep the solution to the mystery a secret until we are into several days rehearsal. Need I say that the curiosity generated does worlds for team spirit?

End the tryout by announcing that those who would like to work on the technical crews, in the event they are not selected for the cast, should sign the crew sheet. You may find names written there which would not have appeared before the session. If the group is becoming involved with the play, most of them will want to be a part of it, onstage or off.

The first tryouts are best in a classroom since the intimacy will allow perception of slight hints of character quality. The individual readings should be in the auditorium where the play is to happen. Ten minutes should suffice for each candidate. The first three or four should be used to ascertain attitudes toward the play and the level of school work. The student then is given a playbook and asked to go on the apron of the stage to read the role or roles for which he seems most suited. The director moves about the auditorium in the area the audience will use and checks two kinds of projection: that of voice, which can be improved as we will discuss in the chapter, "Better Speech for Actors," and the size of personality. Some human beings are very effective a few feet away but blur into vagueness when the distance becomes forty or fifty feet. Others seem to expand with the added space, and their personalities carry strong and true into a large auditorium. This attribute is vital as we recall the ancient statement, "Living theatre is larger than life."

Of the thousands of players I have taken through the tryout schedule, one type always has intrigued me, the Glib Reader. At a time when we see some universities teaching remedial reading, he is even more impressive. So often it is a danger point, because it begins with a sense of pleasure for the director. At the first tryout a voice is heard reading splendidly and the thought occurs, "Ah, here is a real talent, how splendid." Be hopeful, but wary, for often the Glib Reader gives his all at the first reading. The ability to read excellently on sight often has a compensatory side; he never reads any better. Many directors who cast plays too quickly have told me, "I had a real disappointment in so–and–so. He was beautiful at tryouts but never improved. As rehearsals progressed, the mediocre readers developed and many went beyond him. I don't understand it."

More is needed than the facile, the quick, for the intricate process of transmitting emotions, meanings and ideas through the spoken word. One of the general obstacles to good reading may lie in our current passion for speed. "If we aren't at now, Man, let's hurry and get there." One of the sillier manifestations of the fast–is–better philosophy is speed reading. Unless the eye is consuming trivia, where ideas are spaced one in every ten–thousand words, speed reading has little merit. Words of great moment, and literature which deserves the name is made up of them, deserve and need more than reckless scanning if they are to create the proper empathy in the reader.

In the cases of many of the high school students with whom I have worked, guidance toward a slower rate has been preliminary to acquiring basic techniques of the stage. I know many directors have had occasional students who stumbled and mumbled their way in oral reading until they felt any measure might help; if he'd read faster, he might read better. That solution may be no sounder for the director than for the supervisor of student driving who, finding a dullard in his group, might be tempted to say, "Drive faster—faster; maybe you'll drive better!"

In the individual reading sessions, a majority may seem to be reading too rapidly, especially as the director moves back in the auditorium to check projection. There is a definite fall–off in the efficiency of communication as the distance between speaker and auditor increases. You can follow breakneck speech if it comes through a telephone pressed tightly against your ear but that same speech from your stage blurs into unintelligibility before you get back to the forty–foot mark which is the point at which effective communication in a theatre drops sharply.

After the individual interviews, the second group meeting should include the most likely candidates. Two or three may be invited for some of the roles, and everyone should understand that it is not yet time for final decisions. The general level of the readings should be rising because the material now is becoming familiar and self–consciousness may be on the wane. Do not finish the play yet, but read far enough into the final act to include any characters who previously have not appeared.

The second group reading concludes with an announcement that the schedule of individual appointments for the next week will be posted. These call–backs should find a pleasant sense of growth in the readers, and lead to selections for the final group reading. If two players seem of almost equal merit, offer one the opportunity of being an understudy. The understudy system spreads out the training but does consume some of the director's precious time. From what I have seen of the ultimate results, the double–cast has certain faults, the most important being that neither cast will progress as far as a single company could have gone.

If the two weeks have gone well, the director's knowledge of play and players should be enormously increased. While there may be some qualms about two or three decisions, reasonable sureness about the balance of the cast gives comfort. Do not announce the final decisions at the group meeting if there are any "second choices" still reading. Simply state when the cast selections will be posted with the rehearsal schedule for the ensuing week. Try very hard not to make any aspiring player feel embarrassed; it contributes substantially to overall morale.

chapter six

THE REHEARSAL PLAN

An idea much too fixed among those who make high school theatre is that a rehearsal is simply a rehearsal, each one being like another. This same idea, which we shall strive to un–fix, goes on to the rather vague hope that by the mere process of repetition a play will emerge at the end of this chain of carbon–copy rehearsals. Sometimes it does, but any play will benefit from a rehearsal timetable in which every session has a point and a purpose.

It shouldn't be necessary to convince teachers of the value and necessity of a detailed work program, for this is standard procedure in the classroom. Yet something happens to some of my teacher friends when they assume the duties of a director. When I have asked such questions as, "What did you do in the first week of rehearsal?" I have received such ridiculous answers as, "Oh, we just kept going over Act One." An even more frightening reply came when I asked, "What was the object of your final dress rehearsal?" and was told, "To see if everyone knew their lines."

Some of this comes from lack of knowledge, from the apparent simplicity of the theatre process which seems to delude the average citizen. You who read these pages can no longer relax in bland ignorance about theatre, for I trust you already have begun to feel that it is an enterprise of great complexity. That complexity is not going to frighten you but rather will act as a stimulus in the learning process. Theatre is one of the rare and great teachers, a mentor that gives increasingly to us with time and experience. Each bit of knowledge she imparts to the doers has an exciting aesthetic context, as does all sound labor in an art form.

This is what theatre learning should be for you as a director and for the students who follow your guidance in making the play. This demands careful planning—but what results it can bring! Margaret Mary and I as directors often have had the special reward of being told that we had made the rehearsal period so gratifying our players were almost sorry to move into the performances.

To teach in this fashion, as you know, requires complete organization and assuredness on the part of the instructor. The organization we will do; the assuredness you can acquire. At the moment you have two essential ingredients: the text of a play and a group of people chosen to enact the characters. Neither of these is an absolute. The play, done by various production groups, can result in performances of different values. Your students can develop into various degrees of competence, depending on their talent, your direction, the effectiveness of their own work, and the time you have for preparation.

All these are variables except one, the time. How sad that in many productions in which all the variables succeeded, the performance was not as good as it should have been because the director failed to organize and efficiently use the time for preparation. In assembling a television set or an automobile, it is not easy to make mistakes, although Ralph Nader shows us they occur, because certain parts will not fit until other parts are in place. Play production is quite the opposite. Certain tasks can be completed at various points on the timetable, but the point determines whether the completion is beneficial or harmful. The friend who felt the object of the final dress rehearsal was to see "if they knew their lines" is an example. Any play which has that goal at that point in time deserves to be quite dreadful.

You cannot treat living theatre as an art form unless you agree that memorization is one of the basic first steps in preparation. An actor who is worried about knowing the next word cannot pay much attention to the more important points of technique which should permeate his being in performance. This is one more marvelous difference between what was once called with some justification "the legitimate theatre" and its mechanical cousin, television. I'm very glad that cue cards are used in TV; it suits the form. One sometimes wonders how much real comedic talent a man has when he has to read the ad–libs created by his half–dozen writers from idiot–cards so near the camera you can follow his eyes as he reads.

Memorizing lines need not be a major problem in high school theatre. Your players should have active, well–exercised memories from their general academic tasks. They do need, however, a firm hand from you in explaining how to memorize lines and in delineating the exact times when the sections must be completed. Unlike their general work in memory, which usually is pointed toward an examination or recitation, the lines of a play must be learned in three ways. Facts in a history course which are to be recalled in written form in answering exam questions are almost entirely in the area of visual learning. The pupil reads and re–reads his text until he feels the subject matter is memorized.

The actor also uses the visual method in his study but it is not enough. You may find in early rehearsals that some say they knew the lines at home but can't say them on stage. Inquiry usually will show they studied with their eyes but have not learned the cues orally. It is in sound that the cues come in a play. The actor thus has to learn in the second way, through his ears, both the cues and the sound of his own lines as he speaks them.

There have been directors who have taught their players to learn visually and aurally and still found the cast insecure when it began to move about in rehearsal. This results from failure to study in the third dimension, the kinesthetic sense, or learning the pattern of movement. This is the process often neglected. It is not as simple as sitting in a chair for silent study or having a second person read cues which are answered audibly. It is necessary to study in a replica of the setting's furniture arrangement. Stressing the importance of this may induce your people to set up at home an approximation of the furniture used in rehearsal. The player, answering cues read to him, moves about his "setting" in the directed pattern. By this means, sitting down, getting up and all the other "business" can be firmly tied into the overall learning process. Transferring the work to the rehearsal stage involves only a difference in environment.

This is not a tremendous change, but it will require several rehearsals on stage to solidify the assurance of familiarity. This discussion may lead to the conclusion that the ideal place for memorization is the locale where the cues are spoken by the actor who will actually say them in performance and with the real rehearsal furniture, in other words, the rehearsal process itself. Of course it is the ideal location, but you cannot afford the luxury. Rehearsal time is too precious. If you have an occasional player who wants to indulge himself in this fashion you will need to act quickly so that he does not consume time you cannot spare.

However, early statement of your timetable plus the average high school student's facility in memory work ought to make this phase of preparation one of your easiest. You will see that lines for Act One should be learned by the fifth regular rehearsal, lines for Act Two by the ninth and the entire play by the twelfth. This is on a schedule of twenty rehearsals.

As you read the timetable, keep in mind that running concurrently with this is the technical timetable which you will find in "How to Produce the Play."* It is imperative that both schedules be met, or you may come to your opening with a well–rehearsed production ruined by unsolved technical problems. I also have seen the reverse, a technically complete show with a cast under–rehearsed in one or more aspects.

---

* Young, Margaret Mary and John Wray Young. *How to Produce the Play*. Dramatic Publishing Co. 1970.

REHEARSAL SCHEDULE

Rehearsal Number	*Hours*	*Objective*
1.	3	Block Act I
2.	3	Block Act II
3.	3	Block Act III
4.	3	Review Blocking, I, II, III
5.	3	Deadline for Lines—Act I
6.	3	Detail Rehearsal
7.	3	Detail Rehearsal—All Rehearsal Properties
8.	3	Run–through—Entire Play
9.	3	Deadline for Lines—Act II
10.	3	Run–through—Entire Play
11.	3	Detail Rehearsal
12.	3	Deadline for Lines— Act III
13.	3	Run–through—Entire Play (All Costumes approved)
14.	3	Run–through—Entire Play (Lights and Sound Complete)
15.	3	Run–through—Entire Play (Setting complete. Final Props Ready. Makeup Check.)
16.	3	Run–through—Entire Play (Furniture complete.)
17.	3	Run–through—Entire Play (Complete Makeup.)
18.	Running time plus one hour	Dress Rehearsal
19.	Running time plus one hour	First Preview Performance
20.	Running time plus one hour	Second Preview Performance
21.	Running time plus one hour	Opening Night

This is your pattern of preparation with approximately sixty hours in which to take a full–length play from the first blocking rehearsal to opening performance. Many playwrights today use the two–act form which means, in the timetable, simply revising certain figures to accomplish the same work. The initial blocking rehearsal then would read, "Block one–third of entire play," rather than, "Block Act I."

In some situations many rehearsals are held after school when the three–hour session would be too long. This again is a matter of elementary arithmetic; if you have some two–hour rehearsals add enough work periods to total sixty hours.

This is not a magic figure but a reasonable minimum. At the Shreveport Little Theatre we produce six or more plays each nine–month season and performances of each run through a two–week period. This might seem to make the sixty hours of rehearsal difficult to schedule but, by careful planning, at least half of our productions get more than sixty hours.

After Rehearsal Number Three, we treat the text as a whole, a basically important concept. From out of the Dark Ages of theatre, a strange practice continues in remote places of re-hearsing only in sections. You may recall the friend who said, "In the first week we rehearse only Act One, and in the second week we work only on Act Two, and third week just on Act Three." This is dangerous for actors and unfair to audiences. In one extreme case in community theatre, the poor misguided people never rehearsed the entire play until two nights before they opened. I use the past tense for that theatre no longer exists; its demise may have been caused by failure to learn continuity, momentum or any of the vital concepts of an artistic entity.

Among the more pathetic attributes of nineteenth–century theatre in this country were the one–scene actors: players who appeared in but a single scene or act and, when asked what happened in the rest of the play, said, "We don't know—we're not in it." What a travesty in an endeavor which at last has earned the right to be called an art form.

It still is possible to have players who don't know and understand the entire play unless certain steps are taken. It is very important to have every cast member present at every rehearsal.

At the Playhouse we also have most of the technical people working with the play from the early rehearsals. In this way the company works and learns together. Each cast member needs to be given some rehearsal time at every session. It's important for morale.

In the Rehearsal Schedule we have two related, but different, lines of work called "detail" and "run–through" rehearsals. Each has certain objectives and only by blending them can we hope to bring important points of technique to adequate development. The detail rehearsal is one in which the director is at his desk on stage, working closely with each actor. This is stop–and–go, as lines, phrases, or words are guided into proper readings. Pieces of business are established and, at the proper point in the timetable, refined. Relationships between cast and director are close and comfortable.

This is essential, yet some directors fail to realize it is only part of the task. Unless the run–through rehearsal is used soon enough and often enough, the play will have little chance to acquire continuity, smoothness of flow and momentum. The players may not develop voices, characterizations and stage business of sufficient size. A different viewpoint is necessary for these larger objectives, and this is the director's second desk, or table, adjacent to the last row used for audience seating. Do I hear a murmur: "But that would be the last row in the balcony, eighteen hundred seats away?" If you expect a ticket buyer to sit up there, take your table to the top of the cavern and listen to your young people do a rehearsal. Shortly after that traumatic experience, you'll be turning rapidly in "How to Produce the Play" to the section on how to solve the visual and acoustical problems of large auditoriums.

When you have brought your table back down to a place where you can see and hear your actors, and beyond which no spectator should be expected to sit, you are ready for a proper run–through. This demands a complete change of behavior for the director. Be faithful to it, for now you say nothing from the start of an Act or Scene until its completion. Naturally this imposition of silence extends to all members of the company. No stops, no repeats, no questions; the only sounds coming into the auditorium are the words of the playwright.

Now you who have been teaching so avidly in the detail sessions become the learner—and what disturbing things you may learn in early run–throughs! That scene you thought was coming so well cannot yet be heard, that piece of business so effective when you sat within six feet of it on stage is invisible from your new viewpoint, and large sections of the play which had seemed well along now bump and jerk. Those spaces you had been filling with your directing words now are empty.

The importance of the director remaining silent during run–throughs cannot be overemphasized. I've seen colleagues who could not resist immediate correction and so stood in the distance and yelled directions at their poor confused players. This is a double fault. The run–through cannot achieve its purpose this way, and no competent modern director, regardless of length of experience, yells at his actors.

As you watch what seemed so good when you were close now appear so bad, restraint is far from easy, but it is admirable. There is some release in writing corrections on the clip board. At first the notes will fall behind the errors but, I venture hopefully, if our precepts are followed, later run–throughs will require less writing. Before preview time the errors may shrink to a fine brevity.

At the critique the company writes in its own books the corrections you read from the clip board. Crew members transcribe their notes to their clip boards. Early run–throughs may not leave time to complete the list, so the director should say that the corrections will be concluded at the briefing before the next rehearsal and the session ended on time.

The last two words should be stressed. Few points of procedure are more essential to efficiency and morale than starting and ending rehearsals promptly. Each year I hear of high school productions rehearsing until eleven o'clock or even midnight. I resent this because it proves lack of proper organization by the director, and even more I mind the harm it does to high school drama in general. We have to prove to so many parents that participation in theatre is a good thing for their children and that it can give benefits which will carry into adulthood.

Some directors almost prove this and then spoil it with late rehearsals. Average parents accept the hours spent in band and athletic practice as a reasonable price for the privilege and seldom blame them for a drop in grades, but let a student take part in a play, be kept at late rehearsals, slip in a grade or two, and we hear condemnation of the whole idea of secondary school theatre.

The alleged necessity of late rehearsals is as great a fallacy as that terrible old legend that a bad dress rehearsal means a good performance. The truth is that both these wrongs can be charged squarely to a bad or lazy or inefficient director.

Through the years several hundred high school students have worked with us at the Shreveport Little Theatre. By explaining our rigid time rules and emphasizing that we don't want those who neglect their studies, we have had the pleasure of seeing most of the young people not only maintain their grades but often raise them. We find generally it is the superior high school student who is interested in theatre. At casting time we tell them they will have to organize their time completely and that this is a good exercise for adulthood when they will want to be among the leading citizens of whom it is always said, "If you want something done well, get a busy person to do it."

Be certain that the Technical Timetable is followed with equal precision, or you may run into delayed and late rehearsals because some technical item was not completed on time. The benefits that accrue to a production which moves along a carefully planned and dutifully followed schedule are so important they more than justify the extra effort required. Good work may require a little more of us, but it is always worth the price.

chapter seven

THE IMPACT OF BLOCKING

The surface simplicity of art forms can easily deceive the proverbial man–on–the–street. For instance, I'm quite sure that his definition of a director would be "the person who tells the actors where to stand." Needless to say there is a good deal of impressive ignorance in this statement because it ignores the director's total work and it simplifies the process of creating a moving stage picture to something less than window dressing.

Blocking in fact has become a more crucial problem in today's theatre because audiences have acquired a new sophistication toward the sound and sight of actors from years of watching mechanical media. The effect of overdoses of television and movies has been a blunting and wearing down of the public's sensory responses, one of the prices paid for surviving into the Space Age. Hearing thousands of turned–up commercials has done something to our ears, and staring at countless miles of moving photographs has jaded our vision.

The modern motion picture is truly overwhelming, not only

in the wide–wide screen which can thrill us with a face twenty feet high and twenty feet wide, but also in its color. How can the real world compete with the enriched hues which engulf us on the big screen? Between color processes and excellent lighting, the dingiest street takes on a richness of color in the movie which puts to shame the real Gardens of Versailles. And how drab mere humans seem in the poor light of day as our eye compares them to the lush beauty of the women and the rugged handsomeness of the men of the color movie.

The camera eye can keep the succession of visual stimuli constantly exciting simply by change, to say nothing of the advantages it has of using distance, nearness and other photographic possibilities. In the simplest dialogue the film director, in motion picture or television, can build, or at least hold, audience interest by nothing more creative than showing one face and then the other. Sometimes it is the speaker and often the listener reacting. How many thousands of feet of "Dragnet" film were used, I wonder, in showing nothing more than Jack Webb shifting his eyes in the direction of Ben Alexander, or, in the ingenious directorial counter play, Ben Alexander shifting his eyes in the direction that Jack Webb was supposed to occupy off camera. Those are the facts, Ma'am, about the camera; visual stimuli are built in.

Not so with living theatre. The eyes of the audience are individual cameras, in a sense, yet they have but one angle and a constant distance. Nothing can happen at the viewing end to give variety or to add interest; the entire responsibility rests with the director and his players. As a result it is much more difficult to make audiences hear what we are saying in theatre today and harder to get them excited about what they see on our stages than it was in the quieter and slower world of fifty years ago. That we can make them listen and look as well and as often as they do is a great tribute to the higher artistic standards and improved techniques of modern theatre.

This should be a graphic illustration that two people sitting on a stage and talking to each other for ten minutes without doing anything visually is very apt to bore your audience, that the one scene may hurt their reception of the entire play. Even on

Broadway, when we see a director's guiding hand commit such a dangerous lapse of stimuli upon occasion, we wonder why he took the risk. We whose players may be less expert cannot afford to take such a chance.

When a director begins to think about blocking, the concept of "roughing in" is quite useful. I rather like the term because it indicates, as in its more common usage by craftsmen, the establishing of basic forms and patterns. The carpenter roughs–in the form of the house with his framing and the electrician accomplishes the same purpose with placement of conduits and establishment of points of connection and outlets. The painter means about the same thing by "initial covering of the canvas." I stress this because too often beginning directors try to give players material they are not prepared to absorb. Overwhelming the actor with too many details of movement and business while he is still learning to read lines from the book in his hand can only lead to confusion and damaging delay to memorization.

At first it is enough if the student understands that on this line he moves from here to there. *Why* he does it and the exact *how* come later when he is ready for the more intricate phases of learning. I have seen directors of short experience going into infinite detail about the motivation of a cross when the poor player was still unsure of the pronunciation of his words. It gives the director, so he apparently, thinks, a chance to display how much he knows about the play, but it will deter the production from moving as far toward completion as it should.

With the company assembled for briefing at the first blocking rehearsal, the director should explain the geography of the scene. The area used will be the size of the floor plan of the setting and within it are divisions of space which aid the designing of positions which will most ably project the visual impact of the text. In theatre, all directions are related to the actor as he faces the audience, so that Stage Right is to his right and Stage Left to his left. Down Stage is toward the curtain line and Up Stage toward the back wall. ("Above" and "Below" also mean to move in these directions).

Newcomers to theatre sometimes have trouble remembering Up and Down stage so there is a bit of architectural history which helps solidify the terms. In the Renaissance, a number of theatres were built and most of them had raked stages; they rose from the footlights to the back wall, sometimes rather sharply. On such a stage a player moving toward the back wall actually walked "up" and, reversing directions, he walked "down." Some experimental productions today use raked stages, although it seems to me that players are apt to be uncomfortable moving on a hillside.

Using Right, Left, Center, Up and Down we divide our acting area into fifteen points of location. They include: Up Right, Up Center, Up Left, Right Center, Center, Left Center, and Down Right, Down Center and Down Left. Of course we use specific points within each area as we move our players about, but the divisions are useful as we begin to "rough–in" our blocking. A diagram is helpful if you reproduce it in chalk or with masking tape on the rehearsal floor.

CHART OF STAGE POSITIONS

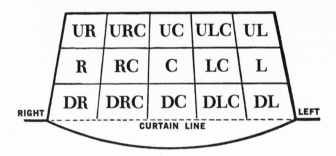

Have your people use stage shorthand as they note your directions in their books. This is a simple device to save unnecessary time in writing. We use the first letters of the designated stage areas so that "Left Center" is written by the actor in his book as but two letters, "L.C." "Cross" becomes "X" and thus a move which you might speak as "Cross Down Right" is noted by the player in three letters, "X D R." Agreement by the company on letters to indicate pieces of furniture saves further time and reduces such a note of direction as "Cross above sofa to telephone" to "X A S to T."

Encourage your people to write the basic direction clearly the first time so you won't have to stop the next time through and repeat the work. A good deal of patience on your part is important, as it will be all through the preparation. Blocking can be not only educational, but also exciting, for the entire company, since everyone connected with the play should be in continuous attendance at these rehearsals. I have found the best way is to provide chairs for them on the curtain line of the stage on a line with your table facing the acting area. The same arrangement can be made in a room, if that is where you are holding the rehearsal. It is a good idea never to allow actors to sit behind the director in the auditorium because their attention is more constant if they are part of the working center.

Since our present duty is basic movement, I know you want to ask, "Do we use the stage directions as printed in the playbook?" The answer is: if the play has been done on Broadway by a good director you are very apt to have a movement pattern which will be quite satisfactory. After all, he worked long weeks in rehearsal and on the road with both the playwright and the designer to find the most effective moves to satisfy the demands of the text and to use well the setting. In many playbooks you will find duplicate pieces of business, a rise for a character printed in parenthesis by a certain line and, half a page or so further on, another rise with no sit between. This means only that the New York stage manager in transcribing directions into his manuscript noted both the original and a second decision for the particular piece of business. Editing failed to remove the unneeded direction, and so you have a choice which you can make after trying both.

Don't be reticent about following the printed directions; this is a way to "cover your canvas." Later you will find infinite possibilities will come to you to give variation and interest. Should inspiration come to you later for major changes in basic blocking, you happily will discover that it is quite easily done, once your cast has been led far enough along the road of preparation.

Keep in mind as you cover your canvas that you should use all of your setting and all of the furniture. Vertical movement on stage is even more exciting to the spectator than horizontal, probably because it is less common in real life. Platforms are not used enough in high school theatre, but the value they have for directing is great. Don't place unused chairs or sofas in a proscenium setting. Audiences vaguely feel that all the furniture up there has a meaning and therefore should be used in the action of the play. We don't blame them for this. It is further evidence that a theatre audience wants to believe that everything which they see on stage has meaning. We are grateful for this belief and, as directors, we ought not betray it.

If you will ponder those last two sentences a moment, you quickly will accept the next premise; any visual element in a play which does not belong in the meaning is likely to be harmful. If a player moves his arm, the audience expects it to have significance such as amplification of a line reading, addition to characterization or reaction. If a player scratches his head, wiggles his foot, nods his head, there is this same search for meaning.

You see my point. The director in secondary school has the formidable chore of removing from his play all the meaningless movement which is likely to be in abundance because of the vitality of the actors. To firmly clinch this premise, may I report that I have attended some high school performances at which I could not see the play because the stage continuously was filled with a sea of wiggling arms, legs, heads and people.

The human mechanism is poorly suited to the enjoyment of living theatre. The keystone of the whole process is the work of the playwright which has to come into our ears through the voices of the actors and yet, as human beings, we are bound to look before we listen. The ear is subject to the eye, so that any movement on stage right will get our immediate attention even though the key speech of the act is being spoken on stage left. This partly is due to the narrowness of the beam of effective vision. The diameter increases with distance from the subject so that spectators thirty feet from the stage can see effectively perhaps a third or half the setting. But as we move closer that little spotlight of clear vision becomes thinner until in the first rows of seats we see a circle not more than five or six feet in diameter.

Are we in full agreement that the director does more than "tell the actors where to stand?" In blocking alone he must create a constantly changing series of stage pictures, each with enough value to make today's jaded eyes follow them with interest and, we hope, with pleasure. To compound the difficulties, within the series he must direct the beams of effective vision to the one place on stage which is the center of interest. At times it may be the movement of a hand, a smile or a tiny prop, and always, or nearly always, this is located with the speaker. Thus visual reaction by the listening actors in a scene has to be controlled carefully so that it amplifies but does not dissipate the meaning of the moment.

All of this gives you the answer to the question which is certain to come, "What do I do in the scene when I am not speaking? I feel so self–conscious." Once your players understand the center–of–attention principle, tell them that they do nothing when they are not speaking except listen completely in character, react inwardly to the emotion of the moment, and outwardly when visual reaction belongs and concentrate intensely so that the next speech will be made with a properly picked up cue and the best possible reading.

It behooves us to involve the entire company as early and as often and as completely as we can. The briefing before each rehearsal and the critique which follows the work session are excellent opportunities to build group spirit and to improve the whole cast and crew's ability to listen. Our people are told how the noise of today's world has dulled general listening ability. We explain further that the actor has to learn to listen in three ways: first he listens technically, as a player who has learned cues which are to bring from him a vocal or visual response. His response has to be an exact one, not on a phrase, or even a complete word, but best on a syllable, and always the same syllable. This is difficult, but there is more.

Next he listens in character, as the person he is in the play. This way of listening has many overtones for the development of characterization. The more complete and individual this phase of listening is, the more likely is the character to be a particular young woman, old man, or whatever, rather than just any young woman or old man.

There is a third mode of listening that is equally important.

This is a general overall intensity of listening to give example to an audience, for those good folk out front tend to listen no better to the proceedings than do the people on stage.

In listening you have a technique of acting with which you can involve your company constantly. Memorization touches all the actors but not the crew, and, once mastered, can be thought of as part of the launching pad from which the rockets of performance take off. Not so with listening; here by stressing continuous application we contribute importantly both to the development of our project and to the improvement of our students' ability in one of mankind's five senses, an improvement that can last through life. If your people carry nothing away from the experience of making your play except a new power to listen more carefully, more efficiently—what a gift they have received from theatre!

As the memory deadlines are met you are ready to refine your blocking. You will find that additions from the director can be assimilated at a speed directly related to the completeness of the memory work. To the actor who is comfortable with his lines, you can give many new points in a single rehearsal. Now you can explain *why* he crosses from one point to another and discuss the *how,* so that the cross has a special quality, a sense of trueness to the character who makes it. In these middle rehearsals it is no longer enough to "X R C." We give the exact place in the area to the actor and ask him to learn it by relating himself to the furniture and the position of the other players in the scene.

This is a time of more note-taking for the cast, but we do it a bit differently. Since we try to get through most of the text even at the detail rehearsals, we haven't time to stop and let the actor on stage write in each new direction you give him. Because he is working without carrying his script, at least to each memory deadline point, you ask that the scripts be kept handy just off the set. Once a player exits, he goes directly to write in all that you have told him.

If you are giving a player a great deal of new material in refining line readings and business, there are two additional methods for efficiency and speed. A crew member can sit by your desk with the particular player's lines and add the notes as you give them to the rehearsing player. In some cases you may want to go through the particular speech or scene doing the lines yourself. In this case the player can sit by your desk with his script and put in his own notes. Don't be afraid to use this method for you are not asking imitation of what you do but, rather are showing your ideas in a graphic way. It would be a strange teacher of music who could not take the instrument from the pupil and play the phrase the way it should be done or sing the notes, if the pupil studies voice. Of course the dance instructor is continuously using the method of teaching–by–example. It is hard to teach well if we cannot do that which we teach.

In run–through rehearsals where you work in the critique from notes taken, you can often give the additions more quickly by example than by discussion. By this time each player's script is becoming a complete record of full assignment, from the stress on individual words to the position of a hand or a piece of business. About this time you may have to give answers to any who may have suggestions about positions or business. Use all the potential values your players have, most of which become apparent in the first ten days of rehearsal. Once this time has passed and your canvas is covered, you become an artist, adding details, shaping, refining the patterns and movements which will become a great part of the final performance.

chapter eight

BETTER SPEECH FOR ACTORS

In each century since Man began his slow climb upward he has done a number of things for his own good, or what he thought was his own good. Many of these projects had to do with better shelter, more adequate food, clothing and transportation. In the more enlightened eras some talent and energy went into the arts, and man finally earned the right to be called civilized.

In the Twentieth Century the long sowing of the seeds of science burst into a sudden blossoming of technology, and it wasn't long before Man had more machines than he properly knew what to do with. The machines took him into orbit and on various trips to the moon; meanwhile, back on the earth, the machines were moving Man about so efficiently that it almost never was necessary to walk, he could travel at the speed of sound and began to be a bit impatient to book passage on the supersonic air liners. As the machines began to do most of the work, Man had time to contemplate the wonders he had wrought.

It was all so splendid. so admirable, so breath–taking that a few people who kept on listening to Americans talk seemed positively churlish when, upon occasion, they pointed out Man had done very little through the milleniums to improve one of the most important differences between himself and the lower animals: the power of speech. True, starting in the 1920's the idea of teaching speech gained respectability in a few colleges and universities, but often the courses were partially camouflaged by being listed under departments of English. By 1920, the University of Iowa, one of the true pioneers, had a one–man department of speech.

Since then, the teaching of speech has developed until it appears as a department in most college catalogues. A few of the more enlightened institutions require that all students take one or more hours of speech, but this idea of compulsory study of man's principal means of communication is still regarded as radical in many administrative quarters. Secondary education is quite another matter, for while the occasional speech class is present in many high schools, the concept of a department or required attendance in speech for all students seems to many school boards more advanced than manned flight to Mars. From many in authority, a query as to why we don't face the imperative quality of this problem might elicit, "All high school students study speech? Ridiculous! People know how to talk. Give 'em another math course so they'll have something practical."

Now wait a minute. If there is anything more potentially practical for today's world than improving mankind's ability to speak more effectively each to the other, I'm not sure what it is. However, we'll leave that larger problem and move in for a tight close–up on the stage, with the passing comment that those who seem most successful in any field of endeavor nearly always are effective, and frequently interesting, speakers. Did success in their life–work magically impart this gift of superior speech or did the ability to speak well give impetus to the progress of a particular talent?

I feel that, despite the attention given formally by education in the last four decades, most of our citizens today speak carelessly, badly or ineffectually, or all three. If you have any doubts, listen to the world around you. This is a matter for regret from several viewpoints not the least of which is that the voice, involving as it does almost the complete physical mechanism, is often a reflection in sound of physical condition. We are paying much lip service to the deteriorating state of physical fitness, especially as it applies to our young people, but we often don't need the doctor's methodical check–up; we can hear the weakness in the voices.

There should be no surprise that we are doing this to our youngsters, and we need look no further for a contributing cause than the crowded parking lots around the high schools. We have almost done away with walking, that best of easily available exercises! This is progress, this is comfort, but it isn't doing our bodies any good, nor our voices. We have little occasion anymore for vigorous breathing; in fact we seem to be breathing less and less efficiently. What is this doing to our voices? I suspect that each of your students would answer correctly your questions: "What is the foundation of the voice?" and "What is its source of strength?" Unanimously they would say, "Breath" and "Breath control."

They know the answers, but most of them do precious little to improve their own breathing apparatus, chiefly because today's environment works against such improvement. The physical education courses required in secondary education are, of course, admirable, but the two or, three hours a week when the young bodies are vigorously employed and the breathing mechanism fully utilized is but giving example. The practice needs extension into the other hours and days of every week. Yet how can it, in a land where we have mechanized ourselves into physical lethargy with automobiles, escalators, elevators and a plethora of drive–in facilities? This surmise may not have merit, but I wonder if a comparison of the normal chest expansion of today's seventeen–year–olds with those of the 1920's might not show a definite decline in lung capacity.A point in favor of my being correct is the general practice of leaning on the crutch of the microphone for amplification of both song and speech. Loss of the ability to project often is shown when a popular singer becomes helpless when the amplifying system breaks down and, even more pathetic, the difficulty a speaker has when the same machine fails even though his audience is a few–score in a rather small room.

Somewhere on Olympus those Greek actors of twenty–five centuries ago must find this amusing. They could make the great throngs or the hillside hear the lines. The only device we suspect they ever used was a tiny, primitive megaphone.

Can't we elude this formidable problem by succumbing to the microphones to make certain the use of words of our play reach the ears of our audience? Mechanical amplification of living theatre is wrong. The most elaborate attempts of touring productions to devise systems for use in the great barns they so often have to play in have been most unsatisfactory. In the first place, living theatre should not be done in places using more than twelve–hundred seats. That's with professional players. Secondly, interposing a machine between play and audience destroys that priceless ingredient, true human contact.

Forgetting amplification and using only the area in our auditorium within the limits of effective communication, let us proceed to the task of building breath capacity and control so that we can attain sufficient projection. It will not be easy in a few short weeks to correct the inadequate use of the breathing mechanism for fifteen to seventeen years, yet it isn't quite that long. Observation of babies and their magnificent ability to project makes us realize that, if an adult could, proportionately for his size, yell or cry as loudly as can the infant, the amplification industry might not be as busy as it is. The baby, using his body without inhibition in full support of total lung capacity, creates sound as impressive as it may be ear–splitting.

During your first rehearsals it is well to take some time to work on this vital matter. You can tell the company quite honestly that daily practice on breathing and breath control not only will make sufficient projection of their play possible but also may well give them another good habit to carry on into adulthood.. With the company in a semi–circle facing you, use these exercises:

1. Inhale on a four count; exhale on an eight count. Repeat ten times.
2. Inhale on a four count; exhale on a five count speaking the vowels: A — E — I — O — U.
3. Inhale on a four count; exhale speaking the numbers from one to ten.

Most of them won't be able to get all ten numbers in for several days. In fact, keep the breathing session rather short for the first few rehearsals for some of your youngsters may feel faint from inhaling such unusual quantities of oxygen. Encourage them to do these exercises at home once a day, and suggest that the first can be practiced whenever walking, using steps for the four–count inhalation and again for the eight–count exhalation. You can add a further motivation by saying that if they practice faithfully they may be able to increase the exhalation count in a couple of weeks to ten. As they become aware of total lung capacity and conscious of the diaphragm at work, better breathing can begin to be a habit.

At a later rehearsal discuss the use to which they will put this increase in breath capacity and control, the strengthening of their voices. Proper preparation in theatre is not yelling but is rather having sufficient and proper energy with an adequate supply of breath to carry words naturally to the furthest member of the audience. A simple device to start building projection is to ask them to read aloud or in a stage–whisper at home for ten minutes a day. This is to take place in a room by themselves, and the material is to be anything they wish but not their lines in the play. Tell them they can double the use of the time if they read some school assignment. Objective: to read with more force each day, without straining the voice, and to use no more words in a phrase than the inhalation can comfortably supply.

Now that we have started work on improving the vocal engine and increasing its fuel supply, let us consider the contents the voice rocket will carry when it takes off. Start with a new dictionary on your table at the first rehearsal and encourage their inquiries about meanings and pronunciations by looking up and discussing some words in the text which may puzzle you. Most plays have a series of words and phrases peculiar to the subject matter which are outside the students' general knowledge. Have them write in simple phonetics the new words and their meanings in the playbooks they carry. These then become an immediate part of the learning process.

Most of the plays you do will be written in the American language so that if there is a dictionary choice, take the one in common usage in our country, not the British. Assure them that affectation in stage speech is no more pleasing than it is in real life, unless affectation is part of a characterization. Naturalness in the speech of our players is essential to moving toward creative reality, and yet it is a naturalness far different from that of two people chatting in a school corridor.

With agreement on pronunciation, we are ready to impart to the lines the color and excitement which has to be present in good stage dialogue. Here again we run head–on into several road–blocks created by today's mores. One is strongest perhaps in the teen–age years; the desire to be a devout conformist. It is so important in high school that we not only dress like the crowd but that we talk like it, even to the point of keeping abreast of the latest "hip" words and phrases. This does not affect our project nearly as much as the way in which high school students talk in relation to pitch, stress and length of sounds.

The use of an extremely limited pitch range is not confined to our high school students. Most adults go through life talking on two or three notes, a good many settling for the monotone. The very wide pitch range of the British is really more of a difference, when compared to our speech, than is pronunciation. Perhaps as a nation we've been too much in a hurry to take the time to range the voiced scale, but in theatre we need every advantage variety in pitch can give us.

As you know, we tend to speak words as we hear them, but the more subtle factors of pitch, stress and lengths of sounds do not impose themselves readily upon a people. It has been noted that more than forty years of recorded and broadcast words greatly have diminished regional differences in pronunciation and have brought some leveling of voice qualities and speech patterns, but the result is not sufficient for the best theatre practice. We need to stir up awareness and sharpen our hearing if we are to have full advantage of the stimulating possibilities of the human voice. Your young people hardly can imagine a world in which you could not hear the sound of voices from around the world and yet, before Edison and Marconi, a man in one place had no sure way of knowing the pronunciation of a proper name in another place unless someone came from there and said it for him.

The quickest way to make your point about pitch and its possibilities is with sound, and two or three minutes of one of the good play recordings will reveal the wide tonal values used by fine actors. This played adjacent to a taping of one or two scenes from one of your early rehearsals should make a blunt illustration. As the cast hears the added meaning and increased interest which comes with variety of pitch, they should be eager to explore this new dimension. Here are two simple exercises to widen tonal range:

1. With the four–count inhalation, sound the vowels with A on the low note and U on the high note. Repeat the inhalation and speak down the scale. Be certain they understand their scale may be quite narrow at first but can be broadened with daily work.

2. Repeat the exercise using numerals One to Ten for the ascending scale. Then inhale and speak down the scale from Ten to One. This will be more difficult than the vowels because we are doubling the units of sound.

In the American language, stressed syllables generally are spoken at a higher pitch than unstressed ones. Our concern with the speech of actors, however, keeps first attention on the playwright's meaning and the constant production of aural stimuli. As you begin to make the point that widened use of pitch adds much to the actor's total impact, you can illustrate the range possible in a single sentence when it is spoken with different emotional values. An example:

"Well, I never thought I'd find you here!"

Use these meanings:

1. Simple statement of fact.
2. Mild reproof.
3. Pleased surprise.
4. Disappointed surprise.
5. Sharp rebuke.
6. Sarcasm.
7. Utter disgust.
8. Deep anger.

If these are well–spoken, each will be in an almost separate key, starting and ending at a different pitch level. Number One should be in the individual's optimum pitch level, from which the others will vary.

One of the most common defects in the spoken American language is lack of variance in the time rate, a fault not only of the general public but prevalent also among many who earn their livelihood by talking. We will assume that as a teacher you are not guilty, but did you ever have a teacher in your school years whose material was excellent, carefully prepared and well organized but whose class for you was deadly dull? You may have felt you were to blame and may have tried to double your concentration only to find that it was hard to keep awake. Could we but have taped one of these lectures and play it for you now, you might well hear that enemy of interest, that destroyer of concentration, the constant time rate, one word following another and another and another with a relentless, steady and monotonous beat.

No wonder you found it hard to pay attention, no surprise that you felt like dozing, for this monotony of time is a key device used in hypnotism: the voice repeating words in the same time, time, time. In the wondrous construction of a human being, one of the details which distinguishes us from the cold efficiency of the machine is that our power of concentration seems a delicate antenna, so fragile that it requires a series of fresh impulses, stimuli, to keep it turned in an exact direction. The reverse condition, a stream of sameness, often turns our concentration away despite our firmest determination.

By now you know that I feel many public speakers do not speak well enough to be allowed in public. From a lifetime of listening I believe we are focused in on the most common fault. No matter how splendid the voice, how round and deep the tones of the politician, the clergyman, the lecturer, or the newscaster, all the high thoughts, the inspirational material, the exciting facts can be dulled into ineffectuality if spoken with a constant beat. Human ears are not dictaphones. We are not feeding words into a computer when we talk to an audience; we are trying to make people listen in an age when environment has dulled this sense. Ignoring the fraility of human concentration moves toward negation of communication.

Would that those who have the privilege of talking to audiences might, before each occasion, listen to a single recorded Shakespearian speech as spoken by John Gielgud, Orson Welles, Alec Guiness or Laurence Olivier! Not for the beauty of the words nor for the impressive range of pitch, but solely to remind him of the enormous benefits which the speaker gains when he uses well variety of time.

I deliberately chose men of the stage for example. Though many public speakers use this technique well, it is in theatre that failure of its use is unforgiveable. The good playwright labors hard to write the exact word to best express the emotion. Yet the player can dim, yes even destroy, the meaning by clomping along in his delivery, giving equal time to each word.

We have no easy recourse to the usual rules of the speech text which may advise us to "Give proper length and force to stressed syllables" or to "Shorten and weaken properly the unstressed syllables." In theatre meaning is the key to time. An over-simplified rule might be: the important word, phrase, sentence needs more time; the unimportant needs less. Translating this into the world of written characterizations, we see that sound groups which have little value for one become terribly important to another. The magnificent final curtain of *The Miracle Worker* gives Helen Keller her only word in the play, and it is but a repetition of the first syllable of "water." Yet when it is read with the proper time, imposed on the correct emotion, the result electrifies audience after audience.

With high school players you usually are working against life–time faults in this matter, for our youngsters tend to talk too rapidly in real life and seem to have an adolescent affinity for the monotonous steady beat.

While you want your players to read with seeming naturalness of the stage, based on an emotional creativity toward which they should be moving, you may well use a simple guideline for rates of time. As readings mature, have them underline the important words, phrases or sentences, using one, two or three lines to give a scale of values. They will benefit from these permanent visual reminders that these are the sounds needing more time.

The comprehensive problem of time, the rate for each scene,

is the director's responsibility and one at which you will gain facility with experience. It is no better for a play to run at the same rate throughout than it is for the individual to talk in monotony. Keep in mind the general principles of meaning first and its projection. Time has no variety unless it has contrast. Your ride in a jet liner has little sense of speed save on take–offs and landings; the six hundred mile cruising pace has no points for you to make comparison, even the earth is too far below. In your automobile in city driving, you have a continuing reaction to speed as you move from stop–light to stop–light.

Variance of volume is an easier way to contribute to the stream of stimuli, both for the actor and the director. If the company is faithful to our exercises, the limits of loudness will expand for words, speeches and scenes. The limit of softness also can be moved as we become more proficient in projection. This matter of pianissimo in the theatre is determined by an architectural resultant, acoustics.

I'm certain it is wrong for me to find amusement in this involved realm of science, but there is a certain wry humor in comparing all the ponderous words written on acoustical progress in the last thirty years with recent achievements in the field. The "floating clouds" of the new Philharmonic Hall in Lincoln Center proved less celestial when the music played. The vast sums spent to build perfect acoustics have needed addition and the solution may never fit the designer's dream. In 1927, certainly the Middle Ages of acoustical knowledge, the Shreveport Little Theatre was built and architect Clarence King blended the hard surface of bricks and the softer great wooden beams and Celotex in such a manner that perfect acoustics resulted, perhaps to his surprise.

Somewhere between these two approaches is that used in building the average high school auditorium, and the results acoustically are various. If you are so fortunate as to have to produce in a Gymnatorium, you'd better check early in rehearsal and see what, if anything, can be heard of your players. When you sit back where your audience will be and hear the sounds bouncing against the hardwood gymnasium floor and against the tiled or brick walls and back again, you may want to do the production in arena staging.

We cannot hope to rebuild the speech habits of our students in the few weeks of rehearsal, but hard work in the areas we have discussed can bring improvement, in some cases a great deal. Any gains will be of enormous benefit to our play. Any permanent fixation of better habits of breathing, diction, variety of time, pitch and volume will have fine potential for adulthood. Of course the underlying and cohesive factor which transforms everyday talk into effective stage speech is the emotional value created by the player for fulfillment of characterization, and it cannot be ignored.

But listen to how one great man of the Broadway theatre summed up his technique for directing his actors toward better speech. George Abbott, whose four decades in the New York theatre have been a splendid contribution, was asked in 1964 as he was directing a production, "Mr. Abbott, what is your great secret of directing?"

"My secret?" said George Abbott, "Why I make them pronounce their last syllables."

chapter nine

CONCEPTS OF CHARACTERIZATION

One of the greatest challenges of directing is to sense the special values of a human being which match most closely the attributes written into a role by the playwright. Not always is a director correct in his casting choices but if enough time is used and earnest effort is made to match the emotional values of actor and character, the score can be kept high. In high school theatre there should be no feeling of great limitation because of the three or four–year age bracket. Each student is different from all the others, despite the urge to conformity. Further boon to the demands of casting: most students are "character" types, which means they fit more nearly into roles other than those of leading men or women. Movies and television have played a rather harmless, but deluding, game with us through the years; the "typical" American boy or girl is not typical at all. Our young people for the most part do not have perfect features and enticing profiles, but they have assets of intelligence and personality more interesting than those associated with beauty alone.

For us, as workers in theatre, this is very fortunate since seventy to eighty–percent of the parts in the average play are "character" roles.

I hope you believe that each person has individual differences which give him a separate distinction; he is himself and not a number, not a faceless unit in a regimented society. This regard for the uniqueness of each person is closely related to our work in characterization, and is the antithesis of stock company casting in the days when that practice existed upon many commercial stages or in the halcyon olden days of mass motion picture production. Television's late shows nightly tell us that Allen Jenkins, Ruth Donnelly, Edward Everett Horton, Arthur Treacher and many, many more had long and profitable careers in the movies playing, nearly always, the same character no matter what the story.

Of course the nineteenth–century American theatre carried this simplification of characterization to even baser aesthetic levels, with an endless succession of melodramas in which the "villain," the "heroine" and the others were so alike that the actors could wear the same costumes in play after play and, I surmise, reuse a good many of the lines.

But modern theatre is not like that, or shouldn't be. Among the higher directorial assignments is to give each of the characters the unique distinction of a real human being. This requires slow and careful development of that inner quality which the director felt related so closely to the role that it finalized casting decisions. This is a profound mixture of personality, emotional makeup and mental processes as opposed to the visual. If the players are reasonable in size and appearance for respective assignments, the balance of exterior demands can be taken care of at the proper time—which is not yet. Inexperienced directors often try to impose the visual factors of characterization too soon and damage their play just as surely as they do by trying to refine blocking before the cast is ready to assimilate details.

We do not create a believable old man by handing a student a cane and a pair of glasses in the first week of rehearsals and telling him to walk feebly and speak in a high voice. These are really but broad strokes of makeup and, as with makeup on the face, there can be no real illusion of age or value unless the quality beneath is right and true. As with uniqueness, characterizations should resemble human beings by growth from within.

Perhaps you are old enough to have observed this little–discussed phenomenon, that those you knew in high school days change basically very little with passing years. As time goes on, notice how often people will meet after long intervals and say, with much surprise, "Why, you haven't changed a bit!" This should occasion no amazement for the permanent elements of a human being are nearly always apparent by the late teens.

Our real concern in seeing friends after many years ought to be the degree of development in qualities long ago apparent. If we are real friends, we will hope to see that the best characteristics have grown the most. Sometimes the fortunes of life exert unusual pressures and we find real changes, but these are the exceptions to prove the rule. Faces tell the life story, faces which through the years become the outer evidence of inner experience. Thus it should be with our actors.

In order to use time efficiently, it is wise to postpone discussion of character until the actors have become accustomed to their lines and know the direction of rehearsals. Then it is effective to schedule individual meetings to discuss these matters. At these private sessions give your views about the character, background, education, family, environmental pressures and major emotional viewpoints. Then ask the student for any additions he can make from his own study. By your prior statement you give him a frame of reference for his ideas. This might not be the best method to titillate a young mind into fields of further inquiry, but our task is to develop a character within the restrictions of a single play.

As soon as the individual appointments are complete, you may well use a briefing session to speak about the way characters think. Being creations of a playwright, the people he has written logically should think like their creator; this is especially true if the author is one of the giants such as Shakespeare, Shaw or O'Neill. These, and many others, write within thought–styles so specific that the actor who tries to work outside the pattern seems out of tune. Conversely, if the company is doing *Pygmalion* and you can guide their thinking into the impish, Irish, spoofing, satirical pattern of the Shavian mind, your Eliza, Higgins, Doolittle and the rest will find action and reaction easier and more logical; the audience may well get a more harmonious and pleasing entity.

Opposing this is dangerous. If you are producing *The Importance of Being Earnest* you hardly expect your players to think in the style they would use in *The Diary of Anne Frank*. Here is a key weakness in "The Method," that over-publicized approach to acting which is based on part of the writings of Stanislavski. Certainly one should read all of the great director's writings, and I agree that his theory of emotion is best for the non–commercial stage: that the players should feel some emotion in both rehearsals and performance, as opposed to Diderot who said in 1870 that a good actor ought to remain insensible to the emotion he was portraying and to Constan Coquelin who held that the player feels the emotion during rehearsals but not in performance.

"The Method", unfortunately, is practiced by its most devout disciples in such an intense individual searching for, and creating of, inner emotional motives and drives that a production composed entirely of Method actors can seem to be hurrying off in all directions. It is difficult to sublimate the individual searching and creating to the strong single design and purpose of the artist–director.

Now that the novelty has worn off, we begin to hear from a number of Method actors that the idea becomes most reasonable when we admit that most experienced actors have developed a method which seems to work best for them and that the existence of a single best procedure is rather doubtful.

How much of this emotion do your players feel, and can we establish a norm and a procedure to insure its maintenance? We'll admit that we can't establish a norm about an answer which should not surprise since we have emphasized the complexity and uniqueness of the human being. If you were to order five of your boys to march up and down the school grounds in the one–hundred degree heat of an August sun and if they were told to keep on until they stand no more, you would receive five different reports of the suffering. Were you to ask the five to read the same line, "I can't stand any more," none of the emotional values would match exactly. To amplify the complexity of emotional variance, we know that the same player reaches different degrees of creative emotion with each performance.

To see that the created emotion of the entire cast ranges in the safe margin between too–little and too–much is one of the more sensitive, subtle demands of directing. Be not dismayed if one or two of your people have no capacity for building emotional values for the stage; some who are paid for acting can't do it either. For them you assemble with direction, costume and makeup the appearance of a performance, and trust that it will get by. I've seen some college productions where elaborate costumes and layers of makeup successfully concealed the stark truth that there was no creativity beneath.

At the other emotional pole, you may have an occasional student who will feel too much, the emotion growing into reality and taking command of the human being. At this point acting disappears, for real sorrow, real anger cannot be turned on and off by cue as emotion on the stage must be. This is a minimal danger, however, and, if it occurs, will doubtless happen at rehearsal where you can explain and vanquish it.

A deviation of the extreme types is the player who becomes overwrought as his reaction to being in a play. This can lead to "stage–fright," a nervousness stemming from failure to concentrate on the correct matters. Any indication of this requires authoritative action by the director who will find that working on concentration should be as continuous for the actor as practicing scales is for the musician.

Here again we see that a cast which goes into performance worried about memorization inevitably is forced to concentrate on the wrong object. If the mere words are of concern, you may be sure little more than words will come from your actors.

In the intricate realm of emotion, you have a fine opportunity to involve concentration deeply because each actor must feel, not too little and not too much. In the search, keep foremost believability and truth.

In the reservoir of emotional memory, the human being has

stored only those real emotions he has experienced. At first reading the reservoirs of high school pupils may seem too shallow for deep feelings required in many roles, yet this difficulty is but one of degree. Our most venerable actors rarely have come close to such violent emotions as murder, terror or horror, in their long lives, but they have had experiences related to them. It is in this categorical relationship that Boleslavsky worked to evolve his system for using the "memory of emotion" theory. His classic example is, of course, having the player recall his feelings as he once, driven beyond endurance, set out to kill a mosquito. By recalling this real part of his life, he can develop and expand the emotion until it will give reality to his lines leading to murder in the play.

So your people, young as they are, have lived a great variety of emotions and can, through your guidance, find a real basis on which to build the needed feeling. Recalling the situation, the details of environment, the bodily position, the tensions, the facial expressions, all these will tend to establish an inner emotional pattern of the proper kind. Intensifying and enlarging the pattern to the required degree can be done by director and actor working together. Once reached, the created emotion has to be retained and reproduced at the proper point in the play. This takes practice and patience. If, in the third week, the general emotional value of the play is assuming the proper form, you may hope to move into final rehearsals with some success in one of the most valued elements of theatre creativity.

You also will be ready to do that which the unknowing directors are so wrong in doing at the first rehearsals, creating the facades of your characters. Now it is time for the visual, and you add the needed accessories. Many of these are physical, the walk, the posture, the rate of movement, and because they are now logical evidences of inner creativity they can be learned and assimilated rapidly. Also add the required properties, the spectacles, the canes and any other character accessories.

For roles requiring special craft or professional background mannerisms, it is well to have those cast in them aware of the real life sources around them. Tell them, however, if they are going to watch real doctors, lawyers or whatever, they must be aware that much of real life is underplayed and that usable gestures or pieces of business may have to be expanded for use on the stage. To illustrate you can remind them of the various television series which have used real–life attorneys in court-room scenes and how most of these distinguished gentlemen were not nearly so exciting as a Perry Mason or other lawyers played with the necessary enlargement by an actor.

One phase of the visual too often delayed is character makeup. If the face of a player is to be changed substantially, you owe it to the rest of the company to let them rehearse with the character face enough so that it becomes an accepted and comfortable part of the environment. The high school actor, particularly, deserves a chance to become accustomed to any drastic makeup. I once saw a high school play which was damaged seriously, although long weeks of sincere work had achieved wonders in all the major sectors, because the teacher had failed to use the moustache needed in one role until the final dress rehearsal. On opening night the initial amusement shock for the other members of the cast was still present and pitiable harm was done.

There are two final points in this sensitive and vital matter of characterization; see to it that each role makes the proper initial impact and, if you have a choice, emphasize charm.

The lesson of the importance of the first meeting is with us daily in real life. You yourself have said of another, "I didn't like him when I first met him but later he proved very nice." Or the other line, "I didn't understand her at first and it took me several years to get to know her."

These are typical failures to give the correct impression, and nearly always it is an injustice to the real personality which has concealed itself in one or more devious ways. How vital it is for us in theatre to keep this mortal waste of time in mind. No time have we on stage for roles to correct a wrong first impression nor have we "several years to get to know her." This is a director's responsibility: to see that each character on his first entrance makes the impression essential to the role and the play. That audience out there in the dark will believe what we do, and first impressions of each character they meet are far stronger than an introduction on the street or at a party. If we err, two hours may be far too little time to correct the mistake and the best of acting can be blurred. I suppose that was one of the few techniques of melodrama that had validity; there were never any doubts as to the basic factors of the characters when they made their first entrances. Such black and white contrasts are not part of today's playwriting, but we, as directors, need to be very accurate as we introduce each of our characters to our audience.

We've said, if you have a choice emphasize charm. The word may not be definitive; the phrase could be "warmth of personality." The subject is nebulous, but terribly real. It is that radiance which some actors possess and which exerts a magnetic appeal upon audiences. A motion picture star has to have it. In the theatre its presence on stage makes an audience feel warm and happy. In the world we speak of some people as "charming," and we like to be near them.

There is much of this radiance in high school students, yet many tend to repress it for fear of moving out of the norm. Whatever you can do to develop its evidence in characterizations which permit it will please your audience.

How much theatre expects of us; to reveal the total life impression of a group of created human beings in two brief hours, to do this with fidelity to the emotional and visual demand of the playwright's manuscript. This is artistic achievement of high order.

chapter ten

PERFORMING IN THE ROUND

The idea of surrounding a play with its audience is not a contribution of our century; indeed it was first used in the threshing circles of ancient Greece. It reappeared in Europe about the turn of the century but made no significant impression on the American theatre until 1932 when Professor Glenn Hughes at the University of Washington, tiring of doing two performances of his productions in a huge auditorium, cast about for a new approach to intimate theatre. Feeling that there were some plays which did not really require scenery, he decided to try the novelty of the "circus" style with the audience seated on all four sides.

The first productions were given in the drawing room of a friend's penthouse atop a Seattle hotel—a circumstance which gave the continuing name of Penthouse Theatre to the project although it moved to several other locations. Seattle continued to respond, and for three years Professor Hughes ran his plays for six nights a week and for a run of six weeks.

Realizing the potential of the idea, the University responded with the handsome Penthouse Theatre on campus, seating one hundred and seventy–two. Invited to lecture at the University, I spoke in the building and found that the elliptical playing area twenty–four by thirty feet, the four entrances up the aisles and the three rows of surrounding seats, was the ultimate for the arena director. Other arena theatres since have been built, some with much larger seating, but in some cases they have lost the complete intimacy which is one of the basic appeals of the form.

Perhaps the most famous, and certainly one very simply housed, was Margo Jones' Theatre in Dallas. This talented director settled for a small exhibit hall belonging to an oil company on the state fair grounds. In this starkly plain room, she surrounded the playing area with a few rows of banked seats and proceeded, before her untimely death, to produce vital theatre with particular attention to the work of new playwrights. An example of the miracles worked was her initial production of "Inherit the Wind," which later was to fill to overflowing the large facilities of a Broadway stage. In 1950 Broadway had a glimpse of arena with several plays in the ballroom of the Edison Hotel, but it did not lead to tearing down the established proscenium theatres and building them over in circles. Rather the form found its New York opportunity off–Broadway with perhaps its most successful playhouse being the Circle–in–the–Square.

Two of the fine dividends of my life in theatre were friendships of more than twenty–five years with both Margo Jones and Glenn Hughes. These giants of arena staging knew that even in the arena enthusiasm's most lush years I was not ready to ask my Board of Directors to tear out the interior of the Shreveport Playhouse and have it reseated in a circle. Yet in our talks through the years I found myself in full agreement with their basic premises. They believed this was a simple way to have a theatre which was an exciting form for certain kinds of plays and also an excellent training ground for young players. For these reasons you may well consider the possibility of using arena in your own work.

In addition to their opinion that arena was sound experience for young players, both Margo and Glenn felt it was easier for beginners to learn the technique than for stage veterans who had always worked with the several securities of the proscenium. For the older players it is not an easy transition, that walk down into the arena, far from the help of any prompter, with an audience to the right of him, to the left of him, in front of him and behind him. There is no scenery to give a sense of support in the rear; if a costume needs adjustments there can be no back-turning to the audience; he dare not catch the eye of any member of the partially illuminated audience for the recognition of the look would destroy the play for both spectator and player. Truly he is a man in space who must have a firm grasp of certain controls to insure a safe passage.

These controls are among the very benefits which training in an arena space can offer the beginning actor. He must, for instance, increase and deepen his concentration and establish an absolute control of character as well as a mastery of lines and business. Performing in the round develops the necessity of making acting continuous through both listening and speaking. The establishment of these subtle requirements will be helpful in any playing space the actor later confronts.

A Stanislavsky phrase which has sometimes puzzled is newly significant if we think in terms of arena techniques. It is "the sense of truth" and was used by the great director to indicate the condition created by the actor when he convinces the audience that the action is occurring as an actuality, that the meanings of his speeches are real, not results of the player's creativity. A deep sincerity and a conveyed sense of the moment's being truly alive for the first time are important contributions to the sense of truth. The arena actor quickly can destroy this admirable objective by any feeling of the artificial in his voice; the moment the spectator hears lines which sound "like an actor acting," the sense of truth is indeed gone.

An exercise useful in acquiring more complete reality in line reading can serve both proscenium and arena players; it is the conscious attempt to give such full meaning to the lines that the fellow player feels the words are coming from the person and not the actor. In the relatively empty space which is the arena stage, this quality is much to be desired, for here are no trappings to assist, no scenery to bolster. There are but the playwright's words and the emotions and lines of action they indicate. Working continually in "the tight close–up," to use the camera phrase, arena acting needs refinement toward complete simplicity. Here gestures and body movement, as well as voice, need less enlargement from life as contrasted with the projection demands of proscenium.

Of course you cannot grade the energies of either voice or body down to the rather dull underplaying of daily life, or your spectators might decide to walk about observing real life rather than paying money for tickets. If anyone tries to tell you that arena playing has no demands beyond actual human conduct, ask him to look again at the television commercials which feature non-actors and which preface the boring words and actions by the cute announcement, "Of course Mrs. Jones didn't know our hidden cameras were on her."

It must be understood that actors cannot use their average conversation speech even though the most distant spectator in your arena may be no more than twenty–five feet away. The tone of voice is more important than the energy needed for proscenium projection; an emphasis on resonance sufficient to encompass the full room is a logical objective.

While theatre–in–the–round needs an increased movement pattern to project action to all four sides, the size of gestures need little enlargement from life, and subtleties of sight stimuli not possible in proscenium can be effective. Perhaps the prime example is the use of the eyes, a tool the proscenium player has trouble projecting farther than six or eight rows back. I often have noted the camera–director's fondness for close–ups of the listener's face and the incessant photographing of the speaker's or listener's eyes as they shift position. In directing arena you can and should use fully the possibilities of these intimate, but powerful, means of transmitting action and reaction. Well used, this one directorial device can do much to compensate for the harsh fact that only half the audience can see the speaker's face. True, the other half sees his back, and the posterior is not a wide–range acting tool, but you do have the listener's face to use for that other half of your spectators and it can be potent. Be certain that it does not so react as to dull attention to the speaker's words but rather direct your players so that the facial reaction amplifies the moment.

As you begin to block your arena production you find your stage geography drastically changed; gone are the familiar up–stage and down; right, center and left. Here is a space, and in that space you design movement related to points of interest. Some directors like to let their players move about as they feel the need to go forward or away from the center of concentration. This may do for experienced groups when they are in full command of their characterizations, but otherwise I think you had best guide the pattern.

You soon will see that any tendency for actors to play into the center will need resistance, for a circle of backs won't mean much. Even two–actor scenes need beware of face–to–face positions of any length. An essential to logic in movement is agreement and understanding of the exact conditions of the locale. If we are in a room, all the players need to know exactly the details of each of the four invisible surrounding walls. Windows are a special hazard and best eliminated if the action will allow it. If a window must be used, each player has to know the location and size, so that all business concerned with it will match. We can ask much of our audience's imagination, but an actor admiring an invisible etching hanging on an invisible wall is a bit too much. This can be solved, as with other environmental problems, by translation; in the case of the etching it becomes a real one on a table or chest. The difference of attitude in a character toward a familiar or unfamiliar room is fully as important as it is in proscenium with the added difficulty that so much of the room isn't visible.

Exterior settings are not common but when called for require from the cast a sound reaction to the sense of space, air and out–of–doors. This attitude can gain from the special condition of theatre–in–the–round.

An asset of arena stage movement is that all of parts of the area are "strong," as opposed to the proscenium tradition that center stage has more importance than right or left, or that up–

stage gives an actor added importance. At the apex of difference is the realization, as you will find, that the center of the arena is the most difficult to use comfortably. If your actors get pulled to the center they should, if they are sensitive to conditions of acting, feel a tendency to pull back so they can play to each other. Finding reasons to move away during action which is rising is not easy, it will be helpful if you make your players realize that in life we say many things while not facing our fellow or fellows. In fact, this single item of movement can do much to enlarge the semblance of reality.

Be wary of the fault sometimes seen in theatre–in–the–round: the restless circling of players trying to make certain that each of the four banks of spectators gets equal time in viewing each face. This very quickly destroys the arena's unique opportunity to mirror real life and, at its worst, resembles a game of Musical Chairs. In daily human behavior many events are seen over shoulders and some details often are obscured. To this we are accustomed, and we will accept the technique if the emotional conflicts and relationships between the characters are true, consistent and continual. Conversely half our audience will begin to feel neglected if a scene is played too long with faces averted, but the profile used properly will dispel this, a device useful when two people have a scene on a sofa.

A bit of imagery you will find useful is to think of your playing space as a web of emotions and tensions, which will by its changing values move your players about. It is possible to relate the web to the forces represented by the four exits, especially if the text gives emotional values to them. In some plays the choice of an exit, the decision to go here or there, is a powerful element, and you must be certain that the entire company relates to the opposing forces. It becomes a starting point for the more intricate emotional involvements of the arena. As these begin to assume clarity and definition, the actors should begin to feel attractions and repulsions which can be put into movement. You will learn that your web of emotions is strongest when stretched widest; characters throwing lines at each other across the full expanse of the playing area are much more powerful than they would be bunched together. You also will find that while playing so intimate that it would be lost in proscenium is workable, strong scenes can become almost overpowering because of the short diameter of the arena. Arena's possible emotional range is wide indeed!

chapter eleven

BARE BOARDS AND A PASSION

I always have liked the ultimate simplification of theatre as being "bare boards and a passion." Isn't this what the art is all about: actors on a platform creating an emotional experience which is shared at the same point of time and place with an audience? This is the rare and unique privilege which living theatre has provided for humanity these twenty–five centuries. The amounts and the values have varied through the ages. At times the trappings have grown in amount so that they often have stifled the power and the glory which could have happened. There are many who feel that the dominance of the proscenium, with its key–hole viewpoint, in the past three centuries has been almost a strangling device. In the last forty or fifty years some of these voices have cried increasingly for a freeing of theatre, a removal of the picture frame and a return to the platform and minimal use of scenery.

This restlessness with the emphasized reality of the proscenium began to swell in the 1920's. The restless ones said that theatre needed to return to its early conventions, to use the devices of the circus, the ballet, ancient traditions of the Oriental theatre, in short, all the means which would make theatre a show taking place on a platform. Do away, they said, with that invisible fourth wall which remains in proscenium houses even after we lift the curtain; put the actors in direct psychological contact with the audience. Stop the nonsense of pretending those people didn't buy tickets and are not sitting out there in the dark. Give theatre back its directness. The Elizabethan theatre was direct. Have we done any better since?

In our unending debt to the European art theatre, part of our obligation is due those like Jacques Copeau and Max Reinhardt who so long ago illustrated the power of directness. At the Vieux Colombier, Monsieur Copeau used only the architecture of the stage as the setting for all his plays. In Vienna at the Redoutensaal, Herr Reinhardt built an acting platform at one end of a ballroom. On it he placed an ornate screen which served as the only background—the only one, that is, save the endless creations of audiences' imaginations.

About the same time equally direct techniques were being used in a phase of the American theatre, although many of its practitioners may never have approached the question theoretically. This was the realm of musical theatre, a type of production in which America led the world. It has been said that the great success of musical comedy in the United States chiefly is due to the fact that we ask little from audiences except relaxed positions over which we can pour the soothing sweetness of music, dance and color. It is easy to take, it is fun, it is entertainment; but it is also something more. Much of musical theatre is direct, presentational. Those players admit we are out here in the audience; they tell us they are delighted to see us; they talk to us, they sing to us, they dance to us; we respond with much laughter and applause and continue to give the musicals the greatest grosses in the industry of show business.

Those of us who work chiefly in the non-musical forms have regarded this success story with a bit of jealousy. Is it right, we ask, for theatre prosperity to be so centered in a form which is neither opera nor play but a happy mixture of the two? Will those people who pay twenty–five dollars once a year for seats at the one great hit musical ever become part of a continuing audience for "legitimate" theatre?

They might, if the straight play could return to some of the directness and the related excitement it once had. There have been isolated ventures, often with great success, but the main body of writing for the stage continues its fidelity to the realistic fourth wall tradition. The proscenium is especially well suited to the realistic play, for it can supply in full detail all the real places and things called for in the text. It is representational or illusion-istic theatre. That is, it represents life in normal backgrounds and natural behavior.

Non-realistic literature for the stage is growing, and non–realistic styles of production are gaining favor. There are many names for the techniques involved. Presentational or direct staging is also called non-illusionistic; that is, it does not attempt to create an illusion of actual reality. In still other words it presents a story in theatrical forms.

On what kind of stage will such a direct experience take place? Where will we find what we seek, that place where actors may create freely in a space, a space to which they can make entrances and exits with ease, one which will give close and intimate contact with the audience and one which will be easily lighted? Can it be that Shakespeare has had the answer all the time? The platform was used before the Bard, but he wrote for it so well that we have only to watch the Shakespearean stage in performance to see the rich fullness of living theatre when drama is created in terms of action, action which flows freely from one scene into the next. In good performances we see that scenery is not needed, that the visual beauty of the ever–changing pictures of the play provide a stream of aesthetically satisfying visual stimuli far more powerful than any series of settings could provide. Our stationary platform thrust out into the auditorium gains wings from the words of the playwright and the move-ments of the actors; we go wherever they will be gracious enough to take us.

The thrust stage not only is well suited to direct staging, but also, given the scenic possibilities of the back wall, can make do with some satisfaction for the most realistic play. As we regard the possibilities of direct staging on our projected platform, let us remember that there is no solid line for demarcation between realistic and non–realistic plays. The content of the play is not arbitrarily involved with this matter of style. Fantasies such as *Lo and Behold* and *On Borrowed Time* are realistically or illusionistically constructed. We know also that the most realistic drama represents an artistic selection and arrangement of content and details and in its staging, more selection and arrangement of business, gestures, costumes and scenery. Don't let that Man on the Street ever deceive you; theatre is not a talking photograph of life. He may have said that's the way it often looks, but he is wrong. Unless there is selection and arrangement, there can be no artistic creation.

The thrust stage, direct staging, and production without scenery and costumes offer particularly exciting possibilities for high school drama. If your assembly auditorium drives you away to a platform, it may be the best thing which could happen to your play. If economic expediency makes scenery and costumes impossible, a different and splendid opportunity for your production may be at hand as you return to the ancient truth of bare boards and a passion.

Though the projected platform is very old in a historical sense, it has created new excitement in recent years in the United States. We like success, and it seems to me that the remarkable successes of the two Stratfords on this side of the Atlantic, Ontario and Connecticut, did much to speed our enthusiasm for this type of stage. While both their playhouses were adaptations of Shakespeare's Globe theatre, it was the stage built out into the auditorium which gave impetus to the excitement. When Tyrone Guthrie consented to go to Minneapolis, the Playhouse built in his name featured the thrust form.

It also is found in the Euclid Avenue Theatre, part of the operations of the Cleveland Playhouse, and the Ring Theatre of the University of Miami can be arranged to use the form although the "stage" is the floor itself. The Ring, by shifting units of bleacher–type seating, also can assume arena and partial proscenium arrangements. The idea of providing the architectural type best suited to the play at hand, usually the style of architecture prevailing when the work was written, is a good one but hardly a possibility for most high school situations.

Yet the projected platform is not beyond us in many places; some schools already have large rooms with an elevated area built at one side. Extension of this to give enough square feet of platform space is a rather simple building assignment, and the result can bring the desired horse–shoe seating. This is what we are seeking, the actor intimately positioned with his spectators, yet not confined by the defects of the arena. The presence of the back wall gives the frame of reference which so greatly simplifies direction and acting. In theatre–in–the–round we must face the fact that there are always viewers behind us, viewers to whom we must show an occasional profile or they will become restless. The audience's presence on three sides of the thrust stage gives opportunity for full use of the spatial features so admired in the arena without the drawbacks. Exits and entrances are far simpler and much less hazardous on the thrust stage than they are in arena, since they can be made through the back wall and not up the blackened aisles within inches of spectators.

In this discussion we are emphasizing the exciting possibility of theatre done without scenery. With the extended stage, however, it is very easy to use suggestions of locale against the back wall. Some of the permanent horseshoe stage installations have a curtain hung a few feet out from this wall which allows hidden changes of any scenery. This seems unnecessary since changes in furniture on the projected stage will have to be made in full view of the audience. I have seen one or two affluent houses where a circular curtain was used around the thrust stage but I hold this suspect; if we're going to declare for the values of the extended platform, let's not compromise with any gadgets belonging to the proscenium. You probably know there has never been full agreement as to whether Shakespeare used two curtains which could be closed between those two forward columns of the Elizabethan stage. We're certain he used them for the lower and upper inner stages, but I hope not out in front. His plays, and the words of his plays, did not need them.

In comparison to theatre–in–the–round, the thrust stage gives us two other advantages: the simplification of lighting and the loss of audience visibility. Of course, we need deep louvers to mask some of the light instruments used on the two sides of the extended platform; we cannot let the beams go into the spectators' eyes on the far side, but almost half our wattage can come from units hung in the rear of the room pointed toward the length of the stage and the back wall. There will be difficulties, but fewer than we encounter in theatre–in–the–round.

The second gain is tremendous to me, for I am one who has difficulty separating the actors in the arena from the visible spectators behind them. For me the center of attention is an immutable part of the well–done play and I want it there, clear and distinct, from the first line to the last. It may be that I have had unfortunate experiences in the arena, but so often my fellows in the audience on the other side spent so much time wiggling, crossing arms and legs and generally over-acting that the poor players had little chance for my attention.

Producing on the thrust stage asks special things from the director, and it would be well for you to have some exercises in the form before you attempt it for a major production. Students, if they are neophytes, will have little difficulty in starting to learn acting in a thrust space, since they will have no proscenium background to relearn or unlearn. But unless you have acted in thrust, most of your experience probably will have been with proscenium, if not in acting or technical work, then as a member of the audience. To gain a sense of the new dimensions, you should do scenes or one–acts as experiments in the stage form. These make excellent class projects or programs for the Dramatic Club. If neither of these groups exist in your school, perhaps you can put out a call for students interested in drama activities and explore your stage form in after–school sessions. Fortunately, any large lecture platform can serve as your temporary projected stage. Don't feel abused at working under such conditions. Perhaps you have not seen some of the places where Broadway casts rehearse.

Even with all the advantages the thrust stage gives us for the non–illusionistic approach, the question of the new, freer theatre goes even deeper. We can't construct this precious quality of directness, although an awesome quantity of money has been tossed around with this expectation; the quality must first be written. When the playwright does this for us, we can have the most intimate of theatre, our players "bathed in light," with imagination furnishing the settings, the colors, the draperies, even the costumes, and it can happen in a theatre building of any form, even proscenium.

"Along here's a row of stores. Hitching posts and horse blocks in front of them. First automobile's going to come along in about five years . . . Here's a grocery store and here's Mr. Morgan's drug store. Most everybody in town manages to visit one of these once a day. . . This is our doctor's house. Doc Gibbs'. This is the back door."

Thus did Thornton Wilder, on a bare stage, set for us *Our Town* in a completeness settings could not match. He was evoking in contemporary terms the verbal magic which served Shakespeare well in establishing both locale and empathic directness.

Mr. Wilder also used the most obvious device for gaining our two desired objectives: the Narrator. This figure, a recurring one in theatrical history, so honestly and easily ties play and audience into a single entity. With his words, he takes us from place to place and often gives impetus to a scene before it begins.

There are many paths, but the honest ones all lead to the same destination: the ancient goal of a true theatre experience. What do we really need for fine theatre? The words of a good playwright carrying in themselves the direct values we so want; a place to say them where we are near to our audience so they may hear with ease; some lights so that our players may be seen; and talent, as much as we can find, developed to the limits of our ability. At the heart of it we need bare boards and a passion.

chapter twelve

DEAR TEACHER, DEAR STUDENT—
READY FOR THE NEXT ACT?

It seems to me that a contemporary weakness in our land is concern with the Now and narrow concept of the Then. In the arts, at least, we give some thought to the future and its relationship to the present and the past. Of course each generation fondly believes that it lives in the Significant Time, but focus of such small diameter leads often to dulling complacency or to enervating despair.

A rational contemplation of the curve of time should give us some understanding of our place on it, and it may well be healthy to regard the past as Prologue and the future as the opening of Act Two. This broadness of view may at least unsettle the complacent and assuage a good many of the crocodile tears shed by the disciples of despair.

Certainly the latter have more than their share of plays produced, and I suspect their anguish stems from two basic tenets; they do not subscribe to a future, and their idolatry of the past makes today's world seem much worse than it really is.

Writing history is a tricky business as the briefest research into the differences resulting from national viewpoints reveals. Case in point: compare the British and French versions of the Battle of Waterloo. Being human, the winners always have given themselves the flowery words in the history books while the losers often did not get their works published!

A further handicap of historians is that they seldom had time or space to write of the little people, and their own awe of the great often has over–emphasized the peaks on their pages. This may be all very well for students in other fields. Today the rule is to read and run lest one be trampled by the swelling hordes rushing up the educational road from the rear. But for you whose interest in theatre is sincere, it is not enough to know a few facts about Sophocles, Plautus, Shakespeare, Moliere, Ibsen, Shaw and the other giants without relating them to the whole of the living stage.

We of theatre cannot afford the easy approach used in some areas of learning and regard the geniuses of any age as shining through time in solitary splendor, dominating and unsupported. The great of the past often deserve our reverence. In the two and one–half milleniums of theatre's record the giants, I think, loom so tall because they stand at the apex of a special environment, a cultural climate if you will, which was conducive to the growth and development of the type. The same talent, placed in a different and antagonistic set of cultural circumstances, might have found lacking the contributing factors for complete flowering.

The Golden Age of Greece made possible the finalizing of the talents of the Euripides, Aristophanes and other playwrights. Had these same men been born in the Greece of the ninth or tenth centuries A.D., would they have achieved so much? If Shakespeare's birth had occurred in the twelfth century rather than the sixteenth, would his treasured gifts today grace our library shelves and our stages? I hardly think so, for the conjunction of his talent in time and space with the dynamic London of Elizabeth and with colleagues such as Beaumont, Fletcher, Marlowe and Johnson provided the reactors in that particular cultural cyclotron.

Our current space projects provide an excellent object lesson in this matter of the essentialness of many small attainments making possible the ultimate individual greatness. You have some idea of the billions of dollars and the thousands of men who worked so hard to bring about the successful Apollo program. Now that it is over, the relentless evaluation of Time begins, and it may well be that once more only those at the peak of a human achievement will have their names recorded in the permanence of History's page. I venture that perhaps not even all the Astronauts and Cosmonauts will find prominence in the record. For the thousands of talented and dedicated men and women whose labors made it possible, the satisfaction lies in being part of yet another triumph of mutual endeavor. These bright phenomena have recurred through the ages and seem to me to give fine reason to years, and even decades, when mankind apparently existed without moving civilization forward and upward. It could be that this pinnacle of science, the space program, might be followed by a crest of the creative wave in the Arts.

So, is your work in high school drama important to the great theatre we dream of and write about and seldom see? Not only is it important, but your contribution also can have a determining influence on the size and quality of tomorrow's living stage. It coincides with a point in time and space when the United States is developing a cultural environment with vast possibilities and when there are new and vital needs for wide and worthy participation in the arts.

Never before has a nation enjoyed the benefits inherent in the production each year of more than twenty–five thousand royalty plays by high schools. At the moment some of this endeavor is poorly done, little appreciated, and tied to the wrong objectives, but that merely dilutes the potential. It does not destroy it.

Suppose we take the grimmest possible view and say that, in a single year, not one student involved in high school theatre ever acts again, writes a play, or contributes an hour to any phase of stagecraft; is the work a total loss? You might think so, although no such paucity of future participation will ever happen. But suppose it did, and that the only gain from twenty–five thousand productions was that of those who produced or witnessed each play, one hundred were stimulated to want to see another play, and then another, and then another. This minor and reasonable miracle could add annually two and one–half millions to the total American theatre audience, a contribution beyond price.

In your humility, and humility is a grace which increases with time for the truly dedicated workers in drama, you are doing more than building the total audience, for among you and your fellows are the playwrights, the designers, the players, and the technicians of tomorrow's theatre. They have to be there, we have no other source. The special talents may not now be apparent, but recognition at this time is not important; far more vital is your example as a person who makes theatre.

You should understand that the art of Thespis does best when it is well organized and efficient. I want you to understand that theatre has two disciplines, the obvious one being your personal obligation to the play. This includes absolute promptness at all rehearsals, meeting all deadlines, and impeccable conduct. Beyond this, theatre has a discipline of its own, even as medicine, law and engineering. This relates to the finest of traditions which have come down to us through twenty–five centuries, an understanding of the responsibilities of the living stage in the civilized world of today and tomorrow, and respect for the time required to earn a respected place among the makers of theatre. It is no more possible to become a successful and competent actor, designer, or playwright in a year or two than it is to become a doctor or lawyer. Education, internship, apprenticeship and humble initial practices are the only reasonable ways to success. The fairy tale of the beauty queen becoming a star on the stage holds but the soap–bubble substance of a fairy tale.

But, Dear Students, your drama work holds immediate benefits. Hard work on a single play can give improvement of speech, posture, self–confidence and personality development which will, with but slight conscious effort, become permanent and valuable endowments for all of your lives. If you want theatre as part of your adulthood, after schools years there lies community theatre.

In this vast enterprise of volunteer play production, one may truly have his theatrical cake and eat it too. Among the delightful differences between the person of talent trying to earn a living as a commercial actor in the hopeless economic morass of Broadway and his colleague who acts in a community playhouse are these: the privilege of enjoying a normal American life with a job which earns your living, a home in the place of your choice, and all the other good things which the average citizen enjoys in our towns and cities.

And, Dear Teacher, are you understanding the wide potential of your drama work for both today and tomorrow? Perhaps you may learn from your colleagues in music and athletics; they attend clinics in their fields, sometimes traveling far to sit at the feet of experts, but the great preponderance of improving their material is done at home. Both have the benefits of well established structures of lessons and/or participation running back to early grade school years. We do not yet have this for theatre, but let us use well the mechanism of the high school.

Speech and drama classes are invaluable, and where they do not exist interest groups may be formed. English classes are logical forums for extensive development of the spoken word; there is poetry to be read, and plays and scenes from plays come alive when the words are made into sound. While some teachers seem to enjoy reading to their classes, in particular the works of Shakespeare, encourage reading by the students. The result can be two-fold; enthusiasm for the subject matter will increase, and you will begin to know the reading abilities of your pupils. A simple device such as an assembly program can be the springboard for delving into basic talent as far down as the sophomores. If your fellow teachers would cooperate, you could have auditions for readers of poetry or Shakespeare and rehearse the best for a Readers' Theatre program for an assembly.

Would it be worth the work to get some evaluation of sophomores if your sole production is a senior play? To answer with a question: would any of the coaches try to field a varsity team of seniors if he had never known or worked with the boys until their final year in school? It may sound like a three year plan, and it is. The more you can do with and for your young people in their sophomore and junior years to interest, train and prepare them for living theatre, the more apt you are to have senior plays of improving quality.

Some of you are thinking: "This approach to training in depth would need administration approval." Of course it would, and we ought to work for not only approval but also enthusiasm. Much of the disinterest of school administrators in high school drama is due to a complete absence of any public relations activity on the part of the teachers involved. Too many directors have been content to complain about the auditorium, the lack of lighting equipment, the absurdity of using plays to raise money for various causes, and any others which may be on their personal lists.

Shall we stop complaining and see if we cannot state the case for high school drama and then prove it worthy of our statement? The Readers' Theatre program for assembly, if well and tastefully done, might interest your principal very much, especially if he could see improvement, or talent, where he had not suspected it. You see, it is very easy to appreciate the boy who runs for a touchdown or knocks a home run; the successful action speaks for itself. Our field is filled with action, real and implied, but we have to be certain that it is seen.

The methods of building good will with those in power need not be elaborate, and most of them cost nothing. I know of one young teacher who discussed with her principal the idea of a four–year cycle of plays tied together with historical meaning. The plan had dignity and importance; the principal became of great help, and it all went so well that the needed lighting equipment became available. Inviting the school board and their wives and husbands to your play involves no expense but, if they like what they see, may advance the cause of your drama program considerably.

Do I dream of a day when all Americans with talent in the arts will have the privilege of life–long development and enjoyment of their gifts? I do, and I am far from alone. It is a dream that deserves to become a reality if our future is to possess the quality it deserves. The Age of Leisure is almost here, even though most adults feel a bit reckless in suggesting that the Puritans' dictum of "hard work being man's destiny" is a credo we have outgrown. But outgrown it we have with our work, our skill, our science, our machines. Dr. Richard Bellman, a mathematician of the Rand Corporation, predicts that by 1990 two percent of our population will produce all the goods and foods that the other 98 percent can possibly consume. Economist Marion Clawson estimates that we will have six hundred and sixty billion more hours of leisure in the year 2000 than we had in 1950.

The day is fast approaching when the citizen may be shaped and molded more by what he does in his leisure than by his activity in the decreasing work–days, work–weeks and work–lives.

Dear Teachers — Dear Students: you know how I feel. In the arts lies great opportunity for the enrichment of man. For the adult, community theatre offers the attractive breadth of participation; there is room for all talents, all crafts, all training. No wonder community theatre is so popular already, and we can use all who come. Unlike the personal hobbies, which involve only the individual in the effort and the enjoyment, living theatre shares the result of the cooperative work with all who come to see. When the play is good, there are laughter, tears, refreshment of spirit: priceless gifts which no single person in the community could give alone to so many. Together actors and crew can achieve this wonder whenever a worthy performance takes place.

As we move along this curve of Time into the Next Act, let us be certain that you and I so do our work in theatre as to make it still more worthy of its splendid destiny.

INDEX